First Acts

First Acts

A Black Playwright Comes of Age

KERMIT FRAZIER

McFarland & Company, Inc., Publishers

Jefferson, North Carolina

"Drive"—© 2010 Johns Hopkins University Press. This essay first appeared in *Callaloo*, Volume 33, Issue 2, Spring 2010, pages 392–408. Published with permission by Johns Hopkins University Press.

"Snow"—first appeared in *The Missouri Review*, Volume 42, Number 2.

ISBN (print) 978-1-4766-8842-8
ISBN (ebook) 978-1-4766-4741-8

LIBRARY OF CONGRESS AND BRITISH LIBRARY
CATALOGUING DATA ARE AVAILABLE

Library of Congress Control Number 2022011902

Front cover image: author possibly 10 years old; *background* © Shutterstock

Printed in the United States of America

McFarland & Company, Inc., Publishers
Box 611, Jefferson, North Carolina 28640
www.mcfarlandpub.com

In loving memory of my parents
BERNARD FORD FRAZIER and MARTHA DAVIS FRAZIER

Table of Contents

Acknowledgments

Thank you so much to my agent, Liz Nealon, for enthusiastically, tenaciously submitting my manuscript to publishers. And to her associate, Mona Kanin, whose editorial work on preparing my manuscript for submission was rigorous and oh so helpful, as was the copyediting work of Bob Byrne. To Susan Kilby, managing editor of development at McFarland, and to Dré Person, assistant editor, for guiding me through the publication process. Thanks, in fact, to everyone at McFarland for so generously embracing and preparing my memoir for publication.

I would also certainly like to thank all my family and friends who read and commented on various chapters of the memoir as I developed it over the years, writing between, around, and through my writing for theater, television, and various magazines and literary journals.

Certain artist residencies have also been of particular importance. Thank you McDowell and Yaddo and Millay. Thank you Bogliasco. And a truly special thank you to the Blue Mountain Center, for it was there, two decades ago, that I wrote the very first draft of the first chapter, "Drive." And it was also at BMC in the summer of 2021 that I put the finishing touches on the manuscript as a whole. BMC has truly enveloped and embraced both me and my work.

A special thanks, of course, is due to my wonderful parents, Bernard Ford Frazier and Martha Davis Frazier, now deceased. I am so

Acknowledgments

grateful that each had the opportunity to read at least an early draft of the memoir. And thanks to my brother, Dennis G. Frazier, Sr., and my sister, Sheila F. Lonesome, for their continued love and advice. A special thanks to my ex-wife and still good friend, Leena Kuivanen. And most of all, much thanks and love to my beautiful daughters, Eliisa Martha Frazier and Katja Helena Frazier, and to my four beautiful grandchildren, Kingston, Wesley, Anton, and Ruby, who forever inspire me and bring such joy to my life.

Prologue

"Turn around, Kermit."

And so I had. Me looking like a waif in that sepia photo, despite my being surrounded by three generations of one side of my family: my paternal great-grandmother, my paternal grandfather, an aunt and an uncle, and my dad. All of them smiling easily, almost cockily. The keen and quiet confidence of a middle-class Black family in Washington, DC. Or more precisely Anacostia, a section of Southeast DC.

But in that fascinating photo my relatives' smiles are essentially atmospheric, a strongly ambient background glow. The foreground is inadvertently reserved for me, the shy, rather reticent subject of the photograph.

"Turn around, Kermit," someone must have said. Probably my mom, a camera forever at her disposal, strapped both to her sensibilities and her immutable need to preserve.

Kermit. A name my father had given me because he knew someone by that name and liked it.

"Turn around, Kermit."

And I had dutifully obeyed, turned my head as I sat sternly in my chair, hands together under the table between my legs, a glass of milk waiting on the table near my still-empty plate—a glass etched with a cute little white boy, hobo stick in hand, marching insouciant, probably down some country road. *My* glass.

Author at Thanksgiving table in 1954 with (seated from left) Grandpa Frazier and Great Grandma Ford and standing (from left) Uncle Leo, Aunt Evelyn, and Bernard, author's father.

I look pliant and naïve, with sweet lips and a kind of gaze in my eyes that suggests a combination of wonder, need, and incipient fear. A look, however, that's shaded and shadowed by a curious kind of grownup gravity on my brow.

It's the fall of 1954. And judging from the fat, luscious turkey that graces the festive-looking dining room table, we're posing at Thanksgiving. *Our* house. Although I have no idea where my younger brother Dennis and younger sister Sheila are. Perhaps at the other end of the table. In any event, they're missing in the photo.

It's a house that my parents rent from my father's father. George Frazier first lived there with *his* family before moving down the street to still another house he had built. Grandpa, head cocked and looking away from the camera, is seated to my immediate left. And then there's my dad, standing behind his grandmother, leaning with his left elbow on an old, low-rise wooden China cabinet. Cool, calm, collected, and less in direct light than any of us. He appears even more handsome, more provocative and hip, than he normally does—looking as though he were an on-the-road jazz musician deigning to visit his family over the holidays, the bold bebop of Charlie Parker ever looping in his head.

As for eight-year-old me? Well, I wonder what's looping through my head. I wonder why I appear so lonely, so alone, in this fine, familial, before-gracing-the-table scene. I long to melt into the picture, to be that Negro kid at that precise moment once again. But in critical ways all I can do is look—stare and stare into my eyes peering back at the camera and beyond.

How many such pictures generate as much longing as they do details? How many such photographs do we have of ourselves growing up: frozen in time or ever looping through our minds; pressed into albums or fixed in our memories yet ever suing for realignment; faded by exposure, or hidden behind others, or as crystal clear as the light of some new day, some new discovery? How many ways do we have of seeing our past selves, how many aspects of perception? What, in fact, is the right, or at least the best, way to piece the puzzle of self?

Drive

My father drove me. He drove me in our green, squat-looking 1954 Chevrolet, a rounded bug of a Bel Air before that model sprouted wings as though it were meant to fly. He could drive me because he was working the four-to-twelve shift at the Navy Yard so that he could get my brother, sister, and me breakfast and off to school, since my mother was a full-time student and busy with her own crucial work. He was a quiet, conscientious, steadfast father who was perhaps the least formally educated among his brother, sister, and cousins, having dropped out of Howard University after a year and a half, joined the Navy, and become a machinist, working for the federal government his whole life. Yet in many ways he was perhaps one of the brightest, the most practical *and* spiritual, and in some sense the clearest thinker. He drove me because he also drove a taxi-cab part-time and knew the streets of DC like the back of his hand. Drove me down Shannon Place from our house to Talbert Street, then up Nichols Avenue past his old elementary school and our Baptist church, over the bridge past *my* old elementary school, up, up the hill past the hospital into an essentially white neighborhood that had a movie theater we couldn't go to until recently. Drove me along Alabama Avenue for a couple of blocks and then down Wheeler Road into Oxon Run and right on Mississippi Avenue to my new school.

No.

My mother drove me. She had such drive within her. She drove me on her way to DC Teachers College, where she'd just entered her third year, having started college full-time when I was ten. She was bright and ambitious and determined to get her degree, to be a professional, to move up from secretary turned housewife, mother, and keeper of others' children to elementary school teacher, like many of the women of the family she'd married into and unlike virtually any of the women of her own. She drove me in the car she used regularly, since my father owned a black and white '51 Chevy taxicab that he used to take to work. She drove me up what was to become Martin Luther King, Jr. Avenue ten years later, past the decades-old Birney Elementary School, past the Bethlehem Baptist Church, across the Suitland Parkway that had years earlier split the Barry Farms community in two, past the eight-year-old "new" Birney Elementary School, up, up the hill past the red-brick walls of Saint Elizabeths Hospital, into Congress Heights and past the movie theater of the same name, then down Fourth Street toward Simon Elementary School, where she was to later student teach, and finally left on Mississippi Avenue to Hart Junior High School.

No.

My teachers and my principal drove me. Pushed, praised, and pampered me. Put up with my stoicism and modesty in the face of my intelligence. Passed me on with mixed feelings from one grade and classroom to the next. I was their Black wunderkind, their star pupil at Birney Elementary. A school named after James Gillespie Birney, former Kentucky slave owner turned moderate abolitionist, who didn't share William Lloyd Garrison's opposition to political action, who professed loyalty to the Constitution rather than to possible dissolution of these United States, who ran for president in 1840 and 1844 from the Liberty Party, a party he helped to found, one whose six electoral votes in New York in 1844 gave that state to Polk instead of Clay and cost Clay the presidency. A school built for Black children in 1889 that was rebuilt in 1901 and was still a school for Black children when its third incarnation opened in 1950. A school that helped to anchor our community in Anacostia just as the Negro churches, businesses, social centers, and lone movie theater, the George Washington Carver, did. A school with its own orchestra, choral group, and award-winning magazine called *Birney Life*. A school that assiduously paved the way for its graduates to move up and out to Frederick Douglass Junior High School less than a mile away, an easy walk, hardly worth the drive.

But oh, then, oh, those tests, those citywide standardized tests. At least ninth grade levels on all those sixth-grade tests. They were powerful proofs, vivid validations to all their caring eyes, potent fuel for the reluctant rocket that was me. Drive, they said through reassuring smiles. You can drive so much farther on all this fuel, past your classmates and their junior high, higher, farther, up over the hill and into the heights, over the invisible border and into another land, for that's the only place where certain honors lie—indeed, the only place where the top track has been laid.

No.

History drove me, nearly unawares. Began its drive four years before, when the Supreme Court ruled in *Brown v. Board of Education of Topeka* that separate but equal in the nation's public schools wasn't equal at all, that integration had to be instituted with all deliberate speed, a decision coaxed unanimously into being by Chief Justice Earl Warren but only made possible by the pounding perseverance of one Thurgood Marshall, who had developed his civil-rights lawyer skills in the 1930s under the tough tutelage of Howard University Law School's brilliant Charles Hamilton Houston, who was born in Washington, DC, in 1895, the same year twenty-seven-year-old

W.E.B. Du Bois got his doctorate from Harvard, the same year Frederick Douglass died in his Anacostia home, the same year Booker T. Washington gave his famous speech—practical and/or sycophantic—to the Atlanta Cotton States and International Exposition, in which he essentially sanctioned Black people as worthy of separation and almost inherently inferior, which maybe, just maybe softened the blow a year later of the *Plessy v. Ferguson* Supreme Court decision that sanctioned separate but equal laws throughout the land, a ruling legitimized in part by Congressional approval after the Civil War of separate schools in the District of Columbia, a ruling that stood for fifty-eight years until the *Brown* decision, which perhaps led the DC Board of Education two years later in 1956, scrambling to assure that bright white middle-class kids would get their due and have their own classes and thus stay in the now-integrated DC schools, to institute a four-track, ability grouping system for secondary schools based on test scores and principals' assessments, those four tracks being, in ascending order, basic, vocational, college prep, and honors. And it was to that newly laid honors track that I was being driven in September 1958.

No.
I drove myself... Well, not really. Not in any hard-core way, that is. Not in the sense of any abiding ambition to reach some predetermined end, some specific goal, some place beyond where I was, as a shy, good little colored, Negro, Black boy. I did essentially what I was told because that's what one did, that was the good way, the righteous way. I went to school and did my work because that's what good boys, good children did. I don't remember having any particular interest in learning, in reading, in discovering things. I watched TV, played outside, went to church, to Boy Scout meetings. I dreamed. Still, I did well in school because I could, because I was good at following directions and rules and remembering things and figuring

out correct answers and being able to sit quietly enough in class for the time it took to hear and take in what teachers had to say. Underneath it all, I'm sure I was imaginative and thoughtful and stubborn and arrogant, but none of that mattered all that much in terms of *the drive*, I don't think. What drove me beyond my peers seemed to be things I simply achieved, things outside of myself, on bulletin boards and report cards and pieces of lined government-sanctioned paper, that reflected favorably both on me and into authority figures' eyes.

I don't remember saying, *yes, let's go, I want to go*—though I'm sure I did. I certainly wasn't forced. I simply don't remember "yes," the moment of "yes." And yet suddenly, as though I'd been magically transported—flown, not driven—and then dropped, seemingly without a stitch of camouflage, behind enemy lines to mine certain secrets to acceptance and success, there I was.

II

SLAM!

The closing behind me of one of the heavy metal front doors of Hart Junior High School.

SLAM!

And I hadn't looked back as I'd stepped away from the car and whomever had driven me, hadn't looked back as I began mounting those stairs slowly, shakily. Don't look back, I'd told myself. Don't let anyone catch you looking back, showing your fear, your desire to run, to go home again before it all begins, back to your neighborhood, the comfort and security of your Negro neighborhood, the relative ease of being with your own, down the hill from Congress Heights, down past Saint Elizabeths Hospital, which lay like a solid enclosed moat between worlds, Black and white, familiar and alien, an insane asylum keeping the sane sane by keeping them separate, both inside and out. No, don't look back, because no matter who drove you, no matter where you came from, you're here now, alone and on your own.

SLAM!

The cool, clean lobby with its slickly polished floors slapped me hard across the face and then smeared me with a world of white—white faces, white bodies, white voices. I'd never seen so many white kids in all my life—that is, not all at once and up so close without the protection of the TV screen. All kinds of white. Pinks and reds, pales and brights. A rising, raging sea of white. A trembling, threatening tidal wave of white. God help me, I prayed. Please don't let me drown on the very first day.

SLAM!

In the auditorium, sitting stiffly toward the back in an aisle seat, palms sweating, heart pounding, listening to some welcoming speech by some white person in charge yet hearing none of it.

SLAM!

Homeroom assignments. Wake up, wake up, you stupid creep. You can do this. Pay attention.

SLAM!

Down the hallway toward 7–10. My homeroom is 7–10. Follow the directions to 7–10.

I scan the hallway for other Black kids. One here, one there. But none whom I know for I'm practically the *only* one I know in the whole damn school. And none going my way, all nodding and bobbing as I move farther out to sea: goodbye, goodbye, hope you have a nice day.

SLAM!

It suddenly hits me. Just as I walk without falling or stepping on anyone's heels, just as I begin to return to the reality of myself apart from just being Black—the notebook in my hand, the pens in my pocket, the new clothes on my body, the haircut Dad's given me—it hits me. And I feel my first betrayal. Not that I notice that

I'm painfully shorter and look years younger than almost everyone else. Not that I've sweat so much already that my underwear is beginning to stick, and maybe even stink. No, my first betrayal is all too homegrown and lies like a hangman's noose around my neck, growing tighter and tighter with every step I take, as though I'm meekly marching to my own lynching. My first betrayal is that which my well-meaning, middle-class parents have insisted will help me fit in, perhaps in some implicit way make me more "respectable." It's a tie. A damn tie! And there I am, weaving through kids on the first day of junior high school, and not one of the other boys is wearing a tie. Just me. Only me. I'm a stupid, wimpy Negro boy with backward, clueless parents who'll never be able to help me adjust to this school because they apparently don't know enough about white people to know that twelve-year-olds in ties at school aren't cleaner-looking or smarter-looking, or even, God forbid, whiter-looking. No, a tie is just a brightly colored piece of rope a colored kid can hang himself in the bathroom with if the humiliation gets truly bad enough.

SLAM!

His last name is Frazier. F-R-A-Z-I-E-R. Just like mine. *Exactly* like mine. The teacher in 7–10. My homeroom and seventh grade English teacher. The first adult figure I've exchanged more than two words with on my very first day of my new school and his name is "Mr. Frazier."

"Hey, maybe we're related," he says, pausing from calling the roll. And then he laughs, which means the whole class has permission to laugh, which makes me laugh. Sort of. Because where's the joke? What's the point, the lesson? Is he some white father figure sent down from on high to make me feel I belong? Or to show me how much I don't? *Could* we be related? Brown-skinned, wet-from-sweat me and cool, whiter than white he? After all, we're both wearing ties. Is *his* whiteness somewhere in *my* ancestry? Perhaps my father's father's father's father's father. And the farther back the better.

Because there already seems to be enough whiteness outside of me, surrounding me, encasing me, especially since it's now clear that I'm the only Black kid in 7–10, the highest of the two honors sections in the seventh grade, the only government-certified super smart Black boy in all of Hart Junior High School. So much whiteness outside that I shudder to think what might be lying dormant inside, waiting to come out, to exert itself, to grow wild and free in such fertile honors-track soil, to claim me, transform me, make all of my cherished, perceived Blackness disappear, dry up and blow away like impotent pollen from a roots-deprived plant.

And if I'd known Shakespeare's *Twelfth Night* back then, I might have heard echoes of Malvolio, that awkward, socially challenged, betrayed and ridiculed character I was to play with great relish and sense memory years later in acting school. Might have heard and heeded this sad, scary part of the parody of a love letter Maria fashioned for him to find and read aloud as she and her comic cohorts secretly huddled with delicious delight and mean-spirited mockery:

> Some boys are born white,
> Some achieve whiteness,
> And some have whiteness thrust upon them.

SLAM!
Now drive!

III

"Howdy Doody."

The first kid I befriended in junior high school.

That was neither his greeting nor his name. It was who he reminded me of, Howdy Doody. That squeaky clean wooden puppet with cheery cheeks and fine freckles who had his own TV show in the 1950s, dancing and prancing around on strings dressed as an All-American cowboy just like his adult pal and co-host Buffalo Bob and interacting with the likes of Clarabell, Dilly Dally, Flub-a-Dub, and Princess Summerfall Winterspring. Howdy Doody. Not because my fellow classmate in 7–10 was wooden or wore fake cowboy garb or had a weird voice, but because he had freckles and reddish hair and a kind of sweet smile that said to me he was both safe and as naïve as I was. And quintessentially white, ideally white, white the way all the white boys I'd ever known on TV and in the movies and in picture books and magazines and even in my imagination were white. Timmy and Spin and Marty and Mickey Rooney and the Hardy boys. It was as though I was instinctively thinking that if I wanted to make friends and fit in, to be one of the guys, this freckle-faced kid was the perfect white boy for me to latch on to. Not one of those burgeoning James Dean sort of white boys in our class who were twelve going on sixteen. Not anyone who suffered from imperfections, who talked with a lisp, for example, or was fat or wore glasses—which newly nearsighted me had but wore only when absolutely desperate. No, it would be iconic Howdy Doody in the flesh.

So close now, oh so close, that it felt like magically busting through the TV screen and grabbing a handful of "other." Hands, hair, eyes, nose, teeth, breath, skin, clothes. White, white, what's it like to be white? ...

Our friendship was only passing, though—superficial. He seemed to have been more interested in me as a Black boy than as a friend—sort of tit for tat, I suppose—and he moved away after that first year. His family moving away: the beginning of a trickle that over a decade would become a flood. White flight, white flight, away, away, DC's new track system not enough to make them stay.

But Howdy had done his duty. He'd been my test case, my big toe in the water, an important first lesson in my learning to swim with the white kids, to make new friends. White friends. As for making new Black friends ... well, I rarely saw the Black kids. Just in those "common" spaces like the gym or the cafeteria or the playground, where we honors students "mingled" with "the others," moving at times like aliens even in the normal alienation-inducing world of early adolescence. And it was easier for the white kids in my class to hang with those others because many of them were from the same neighborhood and had gone to the same elementary school down the street. None of those Black kids, however, lived near me or rode the bus to and from school with me. It would have taken a great deal of energy for shy, introverted me to make friends with them, and I was spending it all trying to fit into my new special world. And as the days, weeks, months rolled on, I could possibly have fashioned this awkward little ditty.

> Yeah, we're all little pepper specks
> in this big ole jar of salt.
> But we've got less and less in common.
> No, no, it's not my fault!
> And the more we pass by without speaking,
> with hardly a smile or even a nod,
> the more my paranoia hears them thinking:
> Man, that Negro sure is odd.
> And getting odder by the minute,
> maybe thinking he can pass
> from a Black world to a white one
> without falling on his ass.

Pass ... past ... perfect. Only now on a bigger pedestal, and more physically separate, more aloof, more other. Everybody's other. How could I keep myself from being everybody's other? Become blacker, whiter? I didn't know. All I knew was that all of my friends, my buddies, my pals in junior high school wound up being white, despite the potential booby traps, roadblocks, barriers.
Idiot.

Like language, for example.

Idiot.

Words.

Idiot.

Yeah, we all spoke "regular" English. It wasn't multicultural, wasn't the UN. It was just me and the white kids. Unless you counted the Jewish kids, all happily "ghettoized" in the honors track, it seemed. The first Jewish kids I'd ever met—beyond the older sons of the owner of the liquor store two blocks from my house. No, it wasn't about Yiddishisms, or any form of Ebonics, which, unnamed then as it was, my family didn't speak. It wasn't about syntax or slang, about the street-corner call of doo-wop vs. the shake and bake of rock 'n' roll. Still, it *was* about words.

Idiot.

About certain words and their power over me.

Idiot.

I suppose I was just as bright as everyone else. I was one of the best math students in the class, in any event, and I could think, reason, and write well enough. But I'd always been a mediocre reader, slow, plodding, forever frustrated and bored with the process.

Idiot.

So there were words I didn't know that other kids already knew.

Idiot.

And I didn't always *see* words clearly and quickly on the page.

Idiot.

I dreaded being called on to read aloud in class.

"Kermit."

I'd hesitate, mumble, my voice cracking, my body shaking.

Idiot.

Which words would I not know? Which ones would I stumble over?

Idiot.

I saw the word, I knew it.

Idiot.

But I was too nervous and insecure.

Idiot.

So I pronounced it "I-doe-lot."

And the class laughed, a laughter that sounded like mockery, as though I'd finally been found out, revealed as a pretender, a fake smart person, a poor little Black boy struggling to be more than he was, carrying the burden of all Black kids, of the whole Black community, on his shoulders. Isolated and out there, clipped and codified, constantly having to prove himself worthy.

It was embarrassing, humiliating. And it made me angry, incredibly pissed off.

Fuck.

But I didn't say that.

Fuck.

I couldn't have said that.

Fuck.

I could barely think it.

Fuck.

All the other boys could, though.

Fuck.

At least it seemed that way to me. "Fuck" and "shit" and "cunt" and "dick." Joking and boasting and fooling around.

"Wannadicksayhuh."

"Huh?"

Yuck, yuck.

Fuck.

Brazenly homophobic.

Fuck.

I didn't get it at first.

Fuck.

I was such an idiot.

Fuck.

So incredibly naïve.

Fuck.

Such a proper, protected—

Nigger!

No, you don't understand. I'm a—

Nigger!

I'm trying hard to be a—

Nigger!

He'd only said it once, and he'd used it in a sentence.

"Stay the hell outta this, nigger!"

But it seemed to echo forever after it leaped out of his throat and grabbed me by my own.

Nigger!

I'd never been called that before.

Nigger!

Blond hair swept back, blue eyes blazing with anger, lips almost too fat for his face, for his image of himself, as though they'd recently been busted in a fight. Should I fight him now? Stand up for myself, for my race? Shout "fuck you, you idiot?"

Nigger!

On the playground at lunchtime.

Nigger!

I'd been playing Indian ball with other boys, some of whom were my friends from class, all of whom were white. I don't even remember what the argument was about. But since I thought I was one of them, I'd joined in the shouting.

"Stay the hell outta this, nigger!"

Hit me like a thunderbolt.

Nigger!

My friends encased me, stood up for me, while I stood frozen, a mouth full of silence. No words, no spoken language for my anger and resentment. Trying so hard to stay calm, pristine, perfect.

Get the fuck outta here, you son of a bitch. You can't call him that, can't say that to him. He's our friend, he's one of us, he's ... he's...

What? What was I? *Who* was I now?

Couldn't tell, didn't tell. Not my teachers, not the principal, not even my parents. Not one word. Not even when two white friends and I, fellow violinists in the school orchestra, found a note under a music stand in a room off the auditorium.

"What's a nigger?" it screamed.

Just a word.

And then it calmly proceeded.

Just words.

But since I didn't want to know, didn't want to chance seeing any part of myself in those words, I averted my eyes, leaving it to my friends to ball up the note and throw it away. It's okay, it's okay, their faces took pains to say. Nonetheless, I burned and squirmed and screamed like hell inside.

Idiotic fuckin' nigger!

Fuckin' idiot nigger!

Niggerish fuckin' idiot!

Trying to bust through my fear of certain language, cover the distance between me and certain language, the distancing effect of that language.

And the language of distance ... distance ... distance.

Back and forth I went, back and forth, trekking the three miles from my house to my school, informally bused on a public bus, the lone busboy.

Black neighborhood, white school hood.

Black weekends, white weekdays.

Black friends, white friends.

Black, white, Black, white, Black, white.
A yo-yo, a Ping-Pong ball, both ends of a splintery see-saw.
Stop! Leave me alone!

To cope, I'd sometimes shut myself away at home, inside of myself, my shaky, teeming young adolescent self, high, high on a self-made shelf of mystery and quandary and who is he really, forging the barriers of distance and language into a protective shield, my tortoise shell, my way of disengaging whenever I chose to. And I'd bury myself in homework and projects and all manner of fantasies, suitably solipsistic and sexual, simmering with scenarios about escape and power and righteous revenge. Of course, there was play and joy and fun to be had. Boy Scouts and the track team, contests and bake sales, family gatherings and school outings. But for the most part I'd simply drive, strive, not just to survive but do well, be impossibly perfect, remain steady and upright on my fragile pedestal, gathering steam on the honors track, rarely missing a day, studying and persevering and finally graduating from Hart Junior High third in the class of 1961.

IV

At Frank W. Ballou Senior High School, newly opened in Congress Heights in 1960, a scant half a mile up the hill from Hart, one of integration's soon-to-become cliché questions turned itself around in my head like a telling dramatic reverse angle in my coming of age film. Why are all the Black kids sitting at the same table in the cafeteria became: why is that one Black kid sitting at the same table with all those white kids? Who is he? I mean, we know who he is, we remember him from before, but who the hell is he now?

And then I'd reply in some insistent voice-over, squeakily

on-the-moment or in deep-throated retrospect: "Me, me, it's quint-essentially me!" A boy who feels black and white and read all over by everyone around him in a high school at the peak of its integration—in the classic All-American sense of that word, that is, meaning 60/40 white/Black, that last gasp before the tip, the trip "downward," the inevitable, regrettable tumble toward re-segregation. A boy so tightly wound at times that he feels like an entire tug of war—the teams, the rope, the burn marks and the sweat, the push and pull and grunts and groans. A boy fifteen going on thirteen longing to be eighteen.

SLAM!

Welcome to high school.

Shift into overdrive.

Our two honors sections had been reduced to one group of survivors, somewhat strutting and arrogant for new kids on the block yet rightfully tempered by our being distributed among the general tenth-grade population in various homerooms, although we continued in honors classes together. I made some attempts to bust out of my mold as society's cliché example of a sweet-smelling Oreo, but I was an honors-track kid through and through and mostly fell back with the kids I knew, the white kids I'd come halfway through adolescence with, mostly a tight crew of, in reality, only mildly nerdy guys. As for girls...

Well, one of my best friends now was a razor smart, artistic, talkative Jewish girl. At a time when relationships beyond the academic, much less incipiently intimate, still scared the hell out of me, my friendship with her was comfortable, safe, platonic. In tenth grade we deliberately made a slight detour off the track, choosing to take art rather than advanced biology, she because she had a genuine talent and interest in art, especially painting, I because I was, well, perhaps a little tired and needed some respite. And there we were, metaphorically hand-in-hand at school and on the telephone at home, sometimes for nearly three hours at a clip, skirting like true brother and sister a certain kind of intimacy. We were pals, bosom buddies, soul mates, not unlike those Negro and Jewish kids who'd soon be working and fighting together against racism and segregation during those rolling, roiling freedom summers in the South. And I truly cherished her friendship, loved her for being someone with whom I could talk without feeling I had anything to prove. We were sarcastic and funny and finger-pointy. We laughed out loud and leaned into each other, and I felt loved and appreciated and even a little bit, well, self-consciously sexy.

Unfortunately, apart from her influence, my drive to be more genuine and open, to become a more "integrated" person, was less successful than my drive to keep a seat on the academic "A" train. In fact, the former seemed more like spin than forward movement much of the time because I tended to go round and round and round, grasping at relationships like a series of slippery straws, the results of my motion more and more efferent, separatist, a kind of centrifugal force that pushed me downward rather than outward. At the same time, I had since junior high almost unconsciously started down a road toward another kind of disconnect whose characterization finally poured out of me onto the page in one major tenth-grade English class writing assignment.

I liked to write. Even though reading still secretly gave me trouble, even though trying to absorb words on the page as fast as my friends did could still give me a splitting headache and cause me to question my intelligence, I genuinely enjoyed writing, loved what words could do when *I* wrote them down, for it was then that I could exercise greater control over them. Hence, writing was a more liberating experience for me than reading was. Not yet as exhilarating as solving math problems perhaps but strong enough to make me happy to be writing about whatever book it seemed to have taken me such an interminable amount of time to read. Not that I wrote constantly on my own, though. I wasn't generating stacks of journals that I kept tucked away, secret books whose purple passages and tales of angst and liberation might prove useful when I grew up to be a real writer. Hell, I never even dreamed of growing up to be a writer really. Oh, I did write a few very short stories when I was in elementary school and had lots of time, most notably an illustrated serial called *Return to Treasure Island*, which I fantasized about adding to week after week, keeping my brother and sister in suspense as I went along. But that story, like nearly all of the others, remained unfinished, eventually shoved to the side from loss of interest and lack of discipline. Using language, however, to talk about oneself, using narrative to explicitly reveal one's feelings, never strongly occurred to me at all until that English assignment.

Our English teacher, who also taught Latin, was a young, energetic white man in his twenties named Mr. Morano. He was a Harvard graduate who came across at times like an overgrown honors student, a somewhat nerdy, brilliant adult whose body was still sixteen years old, goofy and awkward, his arms, legs, and rather enormous head and facial features, especially his lips, seeming to forever vie with each other for space and direction. In other words, he looked and behaved the way some of us still felt. And as someone provocative and stirring, someone who was the complete opposite of that staid, proper seventh-grade English teacher who'd "co-opted" my name, Mr. Morano could have been a strong listening post for me, an ally perhaps, someone with whom I could have entered into a kind of dialogue that might have made me more comfortable with my own awkwardness. That *might* have happened, anyway, if it hadn't been for me.

Since we'd been talking about autobiography and had read a few autobiographical essays, he asked us to write one of our own, charged us with telling some story of self, challenging us to reveal ourselves as honestly as we could. I was hesitant at first, cautious. After all, I'd gone through life thus far keeping most of my feelings to myself. Why risk it now? But I had to write something, and I didn't want to lie, or tell what I thought might turn out to be some sort of sweet-smelling, sentimental story. So finally, I decided that if I was going to do it, I was really going to do it. I was going to open up about certain things. Especially since I was going to be writing, not talking—Mr. Morano having assured us that we weren't going to have to read what we'd written before the whole class. And so for the first time in my life I wrote about me—or about one aspect of me, in any event.

Still somewhat protected, though, I thought. For as far as I was concerned my essay was as much about style as anything else, about attitude and appearance. In it I wrote principally about my transition from elementary school to junior high school and how being in the honors program had turned me into a Black kid who "acted white" and who felt uncomfortable around those who "acted Black," including some of my relatives. Not my parents and brother and sister, per se, for I felt that we had our own family style. But certain cousins, aunts, and uncles and many of the Black kids at school were too "unlike me" in the way they behaved and expressed themselves. And because of that, a crucial, telling part of me felt viscerally disconnected from them. It was as though the white world had won that part of me over. I explained how weary I was becoming of trying to do something about my disconnection. In fact, I was growing downright tired of even caring, after having cared about, indeed, agonized over it so much already. I recalled, for example, how I'd cringed with embarrassment when our American history class in junior high began studying slavery. Suddenly, I'd felt as though everyone in the class was looking at me, the only Negro present, peering at me with curious, judging eyes, questioning my mere existence, wondering how I ever managed to escape and dared to walk among them the way I did. And I hated that. I didn't want to be different. In fact, I wanted to disappear and then re-emerge as, well, "white like them."

Of course, the tenth-grade me knew how ridiculous that eighth-grader's wish was. I knew that "white like them" echoed *Black Like Me*, the title of one of the few books I'd recently read on my own, the story of how a white man darkened his skin to experience being an American Negro. But John Howard Griffin didn't actually want to *be* Black—that is, not permanently. And *I* certainly didn't want to be white. At least not anymore. All I wanted now was the right to have my own style, the right to create my own self. That is, why couldn't I just *be*, period? Why couldn't the world allow me to feel that just *being* was enough?

It took me a good deal of courage to write that paper, and I was very proud of it. Nonetheless, I handed it in with some trepidation because I didn't know how my teacher would react.

The day he returned our papers I was shaky with anticipation. I held mine in my hand for a moment, then turned to the back page and of course first noticed the grade: an A. I was used to getting A's. But this one felt especially good. I began reading his comments, which praised the clarity and honesty of my writing, making me feel even more triumphant... But then I came upon a comment that trumped all of the others and tore right into me. My teacher had written, "But you shouldn't be ashamed of being black."

That simple, declarative sentence made me want to disappear from the classroom, as though my teacher had just spoken out loud to me. I could barely look at him, didn't know *where* to look, in fact. My face flushed and my eyes began to tear up. But I quickly put a stop to that by inwardly turning first defensive, then angry. What the hell was Mr. Morano talking about? What did he mean "ashamed of being black?" I wasn't ashamed. Ambivalent and alienated maybe. But ashamed? How could he say that? Where the hell did he read that? ...

Then all of a sudden my entire paper seemed to flash before my eyes, revealing in crystal clarity all the bobs and weaves, all the hedges and implications... Mr. Morano was right. It *was* there in my paper, that sense of shame. There in the tone, in the characterizations. I hadn't simply been writing about "style." I'd simply—or perhaps complexly—made myself *think* that was all I'd been writing about.

And now I felt trapped, both by my teacher's honesty and by my own. For although I had physically taken my paper back, I couldn't take back the narrative, the story, the words on the page. Amid the usual buzzing about grades whenever an assignment is returned at the end of class, all I could do was tuck my paper into my English folder and escape as quickly as possible.

I never showed that paper to my parents, but then they never knew I'd written it. That I studied a lot and did well in school was a truism that kept them mercifully at bay this time. But I hadn't really wanted to keep Mr. Morano at bay. I ached to talk to him about my paper, about *my* kind of adolescent alienation. For although I'd written that I was tired of caring about what others' thought, it was obvious that I still cared a great deal. I was too embarrassed and insecure to approach him, however. And although he liked me as a student, he seemed not to want to pry any further. So we both moved on—he literally to another school the next year, I only figuratively, in more ways than one.

Nonetheless, I did try to counter my sense of social inertia in one major way: I poured myself into extra-curricular activities. I wrote for the school newspaper and served on the student council. I was one of the two school representatives at the regional Boys State, one of the four members of school's Wonder High School Quiz team, and one of the five members of the school's citywide first place map reading team—an Army junior ROTC "sport."

I also played two more traditional sports. First of all, I ran track, which I'd done after a fashion in junior high school. Ran sprints and the low hurdles. Not incredibly well, but well enough to get a "letter"—a big, gold "B" I proudly wore on my blue athletic sweater as proof that I wasn't just another nerdy kid.

But participating in sports wasn't just about my wanting to get a letter: it was also about my desire to be more physically aggressive, or at least to find an "acceptable" outlet for my pent-up aggression, not to mention anger. Thus, in the fall of my junior year, although I was only five feet seven and a half and 132 pounds dripping wet, I also tried out for the football team.

My mother was anxious, and a couple of my friends thought I was nuts, but I was determined. After all, I was relatively fast and agile and not so nearsighted that I couldn't see a big football without my glasses. And football was the only team sport I'd been decent enough at on its "softer" level—meaning "touch." Softball morphing into baseball wouldn't have cut it for me the way it did for my brother, and I was the only Black boy I knew who was unaccountably lousy at basketball on *any* level. It had to be football.

That midsummer I spent a lot of time practicing with one of my best friends, a white boy who was also in the honors program but who was taller and bigger than me and had already made the football team the year before. Passing and catching, weaving and cutting. Not exactly punishing stuff, but it had to do. In addition, I began stuffing myself with more food than usual—especially fatty junk food like potato chips and those Hostess cream-filled chocolate cupcakes. It was my naïve attempt to gain precious pounds: I gained all of about two. And in late August, together with a thoroughly integrated group of tough-looking guys, I battered and bruised my way through hot, sweaty football tryouts, flattened so utterly at times at the bottom of a pile of bodies that I came up seeing double and wondering what the hell I was really trying to prove. But I kept at it and emerged in September as the lightest and practically last person chosen for the squad. It was somewhat of a miracle. Then again, it didn't hurt that the white, balding, pot-bellied head coach had perhaps a sentimental touch for his namesake. No, not another "Frazier." His first name, believe it or not, was "Kermit," although everybody called him "Zu."

I lasted only one season on the team as a bench-warming defensive back. But that was enough. I'd survived the long hours of practice, the aches and pains, the falling asleep over homework the minute I opened my books. I'd survived getting cleated so hard in the chin during one scrimmage that only my mouth guard saved my teeth and only my stubbornness enabled me to continue playing, permanent chin scar and all, over my mother's objections. I'd survived entering a game briefly and nearly blowing a punt return, which led me to an evening of extra practice fielding punts in a school yard with my dad. I'd survived it all with the feeling that for once I'd been nothing but this ordinary kid swaggering with the guys onto the field in full tough-kid regalia, from the blue and gold jersey stretched over bulging shoulder pads to the black-cleated, kick-ass shoes... Tough.

And that need for some outward sign of toughness was one of the reasons I stayed in the DC school system's junior ROTC program—required of all sophomore boys—for all three years of high school. Because besides my liking the order and discipline and the fact that a few of my friends were going to stay in the program, too, I also liked the uniform and the rank and the fact that another guy was going to have to salute me and call me "sir." It sort of rang really macho ... tough.

The only problem was that I wasn't all that tough. Not really. Oh, I was tough enough to remain balanced on my academic pedestal. But I wasn't really "tough." That is, I wasn't a real fighter, nor did I even have an active interest in boxing the way my dad had. Hence, the ROTC uniform and a scowling voice weren't always enough. Like the time when as a cadet major, I screamed an order at a Black private standing at attention before me, and he promptly punched me hard in the chest, challenging me to get the hell out of his face. I was so shocked that my sense of authority instantly turned to fear.

I did a shaky about face and walked away from him and into the ROTC office, not just to report the "assault" but also to prevent that tougher-than-me-under-the-uniform Black kid from seeing me begin to disintegrate, my eyes welling with tears at my non-combative nature and my sense of impotence.

I'd felt that way one time a few years earlier when I was shoved almost to falling on the street by a boy in my Boy Scout troop, one who resented me because to him I was this smart-alecky, stuck-up kid, a son of the Scoutmaster, no less, who thought he had a right to have things his way all the time. And stuck I was, afraid to fight back physically and smart enough to know I didn't have his language, his gait, his way of being a Black boy. Back down, back down, then spin away and into myself, the way I did when that white boy called me "nigger" on the playground. It was my characteristic after-the-fact, ineffectual parry—a way of responding that made me feel at times that I wasn't strong enough in *any* world, Black or white, outside of the tiny world the honors program had encased me in, unable or unwilling to speculate that maybe the way I behaved was my essential self, honors program or no.

But what the hell. I kept studying, kept bringing home A's, kept "doing folks proud." And as for going out, hanging out, dating... Well, I rationalized that not only didn't I have the time, I didn't have the walk or the talk either, even though I did manage to go to my senior prom, which simply gave me yet another opportunity to be torn socially.

My date was a tall, light-skinned junior, a Black girl whom I'd gone out with only once before but who'd pursued me as though I were some sort of prize. She simply asked me, and I simply said: "Okay." So it was off to the prom with her instead of the dark-skinned Black senior I really liked but whose father, on our last date a few months before, had laid into me for innocently getting his daughter home an hour late. His barreling out of the house and grabbing her from our cab shook me badly. It was as though he was some sort of predator who'd been lying in wait, although it must have been quickly clear to him that *I* was the one who was the predator. I apologized as best I could. So did his daughter. We pleaded that the time had just slipped by. But he was hearing none of it. His eyes simply blazed with anger. I wanted to add that I wasn't who he thought I was, that I hadn't "done" anything with his daughter, hadn't hurt her. But all he saw, I suspect, were those "thugs" he continually watched over at the Lorton Correctional Institution where he worked.

The front door of his house slammed like the bars of a jail cell that threatened to keep his daughter locked up for the rest of the year. Neither I nor anyone else would ever see her again, and it was all my fault! I slumped into the back seat of the cab like the whipped puppy I was, despite the driver's joking, memory-driven, sympathetic take on the whole confrontation. When I got home I was hit with more embarrassment: my dad had been roused from his sleep and was on the phone speaking—or rather listening—to that irate father, who must have been screaming at him about the kind of son he'd been raising.

Dad was calm and collected, as he often was in such potentially volatile situations. Besides, as he explained to me after hanging up the phone, he knew the kind of son he'd been raising. I nodded and fought back tears. But I never dated that man's daughter again, hardly spoke to her, in fact.

The irony of my sense of what that father had thought of me became more exquisitely clear the night of the prom when, after going to an exclusive club in Georgetown with a white couple—my best friend and her boyfriend—my date and I changed clothes and showed up at a Black house party she'd heard about. It was a smoky, saucy, beer-riddled affair and literally the darkest party I'd ever been to. Everyone there was shocked to see me. I must have looked like a deer caught in the headlights, unused as I was to cigarettes and alcohol and such openly pulsing sexuality. It was as though I'd entered some parallel teenage world—one that my body and soul sensually knew almost solely through song lyrics and fantasy and other guys' boasts.

I hung a bit, tried to be cool, bolstered by the R&B music I loved so much and the one glass of wine I'd consumed at the club. But my date and I lasted less than an hour there, because we were both very tired. When we got to her house, we cuddled some out front in the car. That car being my parents' now ten-year-old snub-nosed Chevrolet. But I was too nervous and inexperienced to do much more. To get out from under, I pleaded further fatigue. Then I walked her to her door, kissed her goodnight on her cheek, and left.

Driving home at four in the morning, blinking and widening my eyes and shaking my head to keep from running off the road, I wondered still about where I fit in, headed as I also was toward graduation from high school in a week's time.

V

"Kermit Frazier ... yuck!"

So declared a long-faced, blond white girl who was both the outgoing vice president of the student council and the senior voted "best personality" by the class.

She was standing in a bright hallway outside a noisy cafeteria and speaking to her white girlfriend as they thumbed through the newly distributed yearbook and had apparently landed on a picture of said Kermit. I'd just escaped into the hallway from the crowded cafeteria, where seniors were exchanging books for signing, and was approaching those girls from behind, meaning to say hello.

But... *Yuck?*

A flash of paranoia. The old what's-wrong-with-me-aren't-I-worthy-enough jitters rearing their hydra head.

Hadn't we worked together on the student council—me being the outgoing *president*? Hadn't I recently won the American Legion Medal of Honor as the top junior ROTC graduate in all of DC? Hadn't I won a ton of scholarships to several colleges? Hadn't I...? Wasn't I...? What? A usurper still? An uppity Negro?

As I passed those girls without speaking, I felt their coldness toward me turn into the heat of embarrassment, but I didn't grace them with a backward glance. Instead, I just kept going, my yearbook swaying in my hand, my focus narrowing to the memory of another hallway several weeks before.

I'd been walking alone during class time, released to go who knows where, when suddenly a Black teacher had appeared, almost from out of nowhere. I'd instinctively stiffened a little, as though I were a scared sophomore rather than a seasoned senior, half expecting her to ask to see a pass, which I didn't have. But instead she simply smiled at me broadly, even winked, I think, and said somewhat conspiratorially: "Congratulations, Valedictorian."

And then she continued on, perhaps wanting me to have time to absorb the news on my own, or perhaps not wanting to add that she shouldn't have told me like that, in advance of some formal announcement by the principal or guidance counselor, but then she was Black like me and needed to share, to show her pride, as she echoed down the hallway, leaving me standing in the spot where the news had caught me off guard, as much shaken as elated.

Had she been real? Had she really said that?

Valedictorian?!

I remember nothing about my valedictorian speech beyond the fact that I had trouble remembering it, so much so that on that hot afternoon in the packed gym I stopped halfway through, nearly in a panic, took the folded pieces of paper from my inside suit coat pocket, and read the rest. Which is what the salutatorian had done all along, he having a keener sense of rebellion than I, he also being not her, my best friend, who would have been second in our class if it hadn't been for *him*, the interloper, a white boy bogarting into the school and onto the honors track in the eleventh grade and then quickly wedging himself between us, not only academically but personally, for he became both a newfound friend of mine and my old friend's *real* boyfriend, and future husband, the three of us, in retrospective fantasy, coolly hanging out together like a veritable academic Mod Squad.

But that valedictorian speech didn't matter all that much really. That whole afternoon, in fact, was just so much icing on the cake, for that morning I'd already delivered one commencement speech, one that I hadn't had to rehearse before my English teacher, one that I flat-out read from start to finish, coming full circle as I did, pretending to tie up loose ends, my past as prologue, my present as my future's past. For I'd given that first speech at ten o'clock in the morning at the James G. Birney Elementary School.

Yes, back at Birney for the first time in six years. Back to where I'd unwittingly become a kind of legend, rumor having it that kids would come into the school's huge, second-floor classroom where I'd spent fourth, fifth, and sixth grades and want to know which seat had been Kermit Frazier's so that they could sit in it, too, and let some of his smarts rub off on them. Crazy, humbling, and more than a little embarrassing. I mean, what did I know really? What the hell could I tell my old school, as young as I still was?

Nonetheless, I forged ahead, stood erect on a stage that was characteristically so much smaller than I remembered.

I spoke about perseverance, hard work, and hope. I told them they should continually strive for excellence and let nothing get in their way, and that they should stay true to themselves. I even told them about my plans to study aeronautical engineering in college, about my dreams of someday becoming an astronaut, JFK's space-race rhetoric still ringing in my head, despite the fact that I was firmly nearsighted.

On fire, I was, caught up in the moment, effusive, confident, proud. And those eager sixth-grade graduates, along with their parents and teachers, were grateful and seemed truly emboldened. And so was I. For I'd been given the chance to return to my roots in one of the best ways I knew how and was genuinely rooting for them all.

Afterward, peering up close into sparkling younger eyes and signing autographs like some sort of local hero, I knew that in four short hours I, too, would be finished with a critical part of my life, that my journey into a broader world along the honors track would be over, done.

What I didn't know was that in three years' time the honors track itself, indeed the entire track system, would be done, discredited, sued out of existence from a DC school system that would be 90 percent Black and collectively groping, only with intermittent success, for other, more egalitarian ways to foster achievement.

And what everyone *else* didn't know, of course, was how much my own achievement, my having "done it," had left me "undone." How scared I'd been at times throughout the past six years, how disoriented and filled with self-doubt about who I really was. For what I'd presented to everyone that day was a kind of persona, an aspect of myself, one angle of perception. Oh, it was genuine, to be sure. But it was also almost unconsciously calculated, designed to help point the way toward success for those young Black kids, help fuel their own incipient drives, while leaving mine ever searching for further fuel.

Snow

For all-too-short a time we were blissfully at one with a white world, one that wasn't "other" when it fell upon us, for it was, in fact, a world of bright white snow that blanketed our neighborhood just as it did all others. A white world to claim, possess, revel in, yet something elusive still, temporary, melting, like the stuff of dreams. A world awash in contradictions. Cold yet comforting; soft and soothing yet slickly hard-packed over time; pristine and virginal yet driven by weather-change toward slush and mush, gutter-clogging and dirty, dark and unworthy. So quick, quick, while there's time, me and my brother and our friends, shouting down the rolling hill through the trees on wooden, Radio Flyer sleds—the snow flying up all around us. Black kids in a white whirl of snow in a Black world surrounded by a white one. Magical, exhilarating snow. One of the few white realities we could safely touch, feel, get next to back then.

It was a privileged sled ride because it was a special hill. Cedar Hill. Special and less dangerous for its being both enclosed and more expansive. Unlike the sidewalks of Chicago Street, down which we usually swooped early in the morning before the neighbors cleared the ice and snow and shooed us away, belly flopping on our sleds one after another from the corner of Shannon Place all the way down the block and off the sidewalk into the snow-covered dirt and grass at the end of the dead-end street, where each of us had to roll off his sled one after the other to keep from being cut by the metal runners

---

of the sled swooshing right behind. Roll off, roll off, roll off, we'd cry. Hearts pounding and laughing and out of breath yet eagerly pulling our sleds up the middle of the street to head back down again and again.

No, Chicago Street was by no means Cedar Hill, which was a several-block trek away. It was, instead, a street right in the middle of our Black community in Anacostia. A street that ran two short blocks from Nichols Avenue, where the 11th Police Precinct stood—old enough to still have remnants of a horse trough and hitching posts outside—down across Shannon Place, which ran several blocks parallel to Nichols Avenue from Howard to Good Hope Roads. A community of row and detached houses for working and middle-class Black people, many of whom owned their own homes, many of which they'd either built themselves or had built, like my paternal grandfather, who'd had *two* homes built over the years, in fact, both on Shannon Place and a block away from each other, the newer of which (1936) he lived in with his wife, the older of which (1916) he rented to my parents. A thriving, striving Black community in an Anacostia that was still, in the early 1950s, eighty percent white and essentially segregated, as was most of DC.

The white population generally stretched beyond Nichols Avenue up Good Hope Road to Alabama Avenue and up beyond Saint Elizabeths Hospital into Congress Heights, down into Oxon Run and into the Maryland suburbs. We lived closer to the Anacostia River, wedged between the hills to the South and the railroad tracks of the old Alexandria branch of the B & O line, across which lay Bolling Field at the river's edge to the North. Other tentacles of the Black community lay across Howard Road in an area initially called Barry's Farm and across Nichols Avenue up the hill in an area that at one time was known as Stantontown.

Barry's Farm was first developed right after the Civil War with the help of the Freedmen's Bureau, which had bought up $25,000 worth of land from the Barry family and sold, rented, or leased it to Black folks to raise money for higher education—especially for the newly created Howard University. Black families could purchase one-acre lots and enough lumber to build a house for between $125 and $300 and repay it in installments of $10 per month. Families relocated from rundown alley dwellings in the central city to renovated former military barracks near their new lots where they could live while they built their homes. In the 1950s, though, the area was known primarily for its rows of flat garden apartments, much smaller than the houses of our community, public housing projects that were called, in a curious shift of the letter "s," Barry Farms—officially Barry Farm Dwellings. An area where, in my view, some of the poorer, tougher Black kids in our elementary school lived.

Those kids came up Sumner Road from Stevens, Wade, and Eaton Roads—those first three roads named for white anti-slavery legislators, the last for a Freedmen's Bureau official—past the recreation center that anchored the huge playground that swept down behind it and Birney Elementary School. My brother, sister, and I would come with other kids up Nichols Avenue, across a bridge that passed over Suitland Parkway, which effectively separated Barry Farms from our more middle-class neighborhood, although we were all at one time also known as Hillsdale. We didn't talk about our differences much: we were simply Negro kids in an all-Negro school. But those differences were evident at times. Although I was friends with kids who lived in Barry Farms, I rarely hung out with them there. And my sister remembers a friend from there coming to visit her and marveling at the fact that she lived in house surrounded by a yard.

Yet wealth and privilege were relative, for at that time I was jealous of a cousin of ours who went to Birney but *rode* with his teacher mother and was "rich" enough to be able to buy his lunch from the little store across the street every single day! And of course there were wealthier Black parts of DC that we almost never saw—for example, way up in Northwest, on the Black gold coast, where all the streets seemed to be named after trees. There resided Negroes from prominent families, more doctors, lawyers, and such, old families with Howard University pedigrees, families who sent their kids to Dunbar High School, *the* academic school for Negroes before integration drained it of its brains and cachet by giving such kids other options, just as it gave Negro kids in Anacostia the right to actually attend Anacostia High School, a mere mile away from the likes of Barry Farms and Stantontown.

And curiously, although Stantontown had a different history from Barry Farms, it had a similar economic arc. It developed over several decades in the early to mid-nineteenth century after Tobias Henson, a slave in the area, purchased his freedom, eventually bought 24 acres and the freedom of his wife, two daughters and five grandchildren, and gradually added more and more land. By the 1870s his family was the principal landholder in that community. By the 1950s, however, although Stanton Road still existed, Stantontown was gone, having been condemned a decade earlier by the federal government in order to build the Frederick Douglass Dwellings, a housing project designed by Black architect Hilyard Robinson, future dean of Howard University's School of Architecture.

But Fort Stanton still stood—as it does to this day—entrenched on a much higher hill than Cedar Hill. Built during the Civil War to protect the approach to the Washington Arsenal and the Navy Yard, it was one of sixty-eight enclosed forts that—along with ninety-three batteries and three blockhouses linked by more than 30 miles of trenches and roads—made DC the most heavily defended location in the western hemisphere by 1864. Of course, by the 1950s there was nothing much to defend against, no more Battles of Bull Run (or Manassas if you were from the South) that threatened the nation's capital (or at least the capital of the North) with possible invasion by the Confederate Army (curiously the Army of *Northern* Virginia at Manassas/Bull Run). Hence, most of the forts and batteries no longer existed.

But there was Fort Stanton in all of its dusty glory—a fort that principally belonged to us Black kids, kings of the hill, who wove in and out of its crumbling, half-barred tunnels. We even climbed up and jumped off a huge earthen work mound behind it that we'd dubbed "Sandman's Hill," rolling and daring each other to climb up and roll down again and again and again.

It's easy to understand why the fort had been so important. For from there one can see clear across the Anacostia River into the central city in all its whitewashed splendor: the Capitol, the Washington Monument, the Lincoln Memorial, and the long, flat stretch of mall in between. In fact, as physically separate from downtown as we might have felt from that point on high, it was indeed a true vantage point, where we could more easily seem to touch the sky

Author (left) with his father, sister, and brother in front of a fountain in DC.

Author (left) with his brother, mother, and sister at a fair.

on starry nights and more clearly view the spectacular fireworks show downtown on the Fourth of July. It was then that the rest of DC deigned to come to us, the streets around the park invariably invaded by integrated armies of the night, bounding from their cars to look on in awe.

We never felt emotionally separated from that rest of DC, though, because we had relatives who lived "across the river" in their own segregated communities. And the fact of segregation didn't constantly weigh on our minds, either. For we did have our integrated moments—such as when my brother, sister, and I traveled daily one summer "all the way up" Alabama Avenue in Southeast to attend a music program in an elementary school in then-white Fairfax Village, or when my brother and I took tennis lessons in Rock Creek Park way up in Northwest. Other than those moments when we were young, we simply knew segregation. Knew, for example, that most movie theaters—even a couple we could reasonably walk to—were off limits to us, that although we could go to Carrs and Sparrows beaches we couldn't go to the more picturesque Sandy Point, that we could only dream about what fun it might be to spend the day at the popular Glen Echo amusement park, and that certain department stores downtown wouldn't let us try on clothes—or if they would, made us use separate dressing rooms. Knowing, however, didn't always keep us from not knowing. Like the time my family went on what we were sure would be a great new evening outing.

Author with his brother (left) and sister.

It had been a relatively short drive from our house, across into Maryland along a two-lane highway. My dad had turned at the sign, slowed to the appropriate speed down the side road, and parked in a line of cars near the entrance. And there we sat, my father, mother, brother, sister, and I, early and waiting, ready to attend our very first drive-in movie. We had pillows and blankets, snacks and smiles, and the need to have a good time at this relatively new yet already quintessential American form of entertainment. I don't remember what was playing, but it wouldn't have mattered. With the big white screen looming ahead, we kids couldn't wait for any old picture to start.

And when the ticket-taker's booth came to life and cars began inching forward, our pulses raced with even more anticipation. A drive-in, a drive-in, a drive-in, as we bounced around in the back seat as

Author with his brother and sister.

though we were headed into a wondrous amusement park. Finally, at the booth, we watched the young white ticket-taker lean out to greet us with a kind of automatic smile that dropped into a locked jaw of astonishment when he came face-to-face with my dad, wallet in hand and poised to pay. The white man—boy really—stared at Dad, then looked away, then looked back again. He hesitated a moment more and then said, in a kind of apologetic whisper: "Sorry, no coloreds."

Suddenly, we kids not only stopped bouncing but barely breathed. No coloreds? But … what did that mean? That is, of course, we were coloreds, Negroes, but … huh?

For an endless few seconds Dad didn't move, and I wondered what he was thinking and what he was going to say or do—eyeing as he was this fresh-faced white boy possessed with both the knowledge and authority to bar him from a family activity he was quite willing to pay for. It was the strangest thing—not wanting our money, not wanting us to have a good time, not wanting, well ... us. And yet it wasn't him, per se, that white kid, for he did seem more sympathetic than angry. Nonetheless ... *what's the hold up, what's going on up there*, I could feel white folks wondering in the cars behind us, as the heat in me, in the car, in all of us seemed to rise precipitously.

Author with his brother and sister.

Finally, my father tucked his wallet back into his pocket and then maneuvered the car away from the window, out of the line, and back down the road.

It was like a retreat, an utter defeat, and was one of the most humiliating moments of my life. As we inched along past the growing number of cars, I kept my eyes to myself, not wanting to see how many other kids were bouncing in anticipation, how many white kids, that is, for I couldn't imagine another Negro family having been as naïve as ours. And even if there was one joyously waiting, I didn't want to warn them, vindictively wanting them, instead, to experience firsthand the rejection we'd just been subjected to.

Yet how could we have known? Desegregation had begun to come to DC in many respects toward the end of the fifties. And a drive-in seemed so logically open yet private—that is, one could be outdoors yet still in one's car, free from outright con-tact and "contami-

Author (right) with his sister and brother.

nation," together yet separate, an easeful sort of transition, an "all deliberate speed" kind of integration. But instead, the only speed we experienced was that of our bug of a Bel Air, as my dad drove away, clearly angry but holding it in, the way he often did with an emotion he deeply felt.

We didn't go home, however, for Dad was determined to find a drive-in theater that *would* admit us. I didn't understand. Why waste time and suffer more possible humiliation? But he drove and drove, never losing his focus or his way, drove in nearly complete silence, his desire and determination set, perhaps his sense of being a man and "head of the household" on some kind of line. And as he did, I began to wonder how long we would wander. All night, all year, for the rest of our lives? Wandering mile after mile all over the periphery of the "capital of democracy," refugees in our own country, searching for a drive-in that would allow us to drive in, and perhaps recalling, each in his or her silent way, that until recently we couldn't even walk into the Anacostia Theater, only a few blocks from our house and on a street called "Good Hope Road," no less.

But then finally, after nearly an hour, my father did find another drive-in. It was in a part of Maryland that was just outside of northeast DC.

As we spied the images on the huge picture screen and the cars in the nearly filled lot, our hearts raced once again, although more with anxiety than anticipation. For there was no waiting, no inching up to the booth. Just straight ahead, then stop, then watch as the white female ticket-taker took Dad's money with ne'er one crack in her proffered smile. And so in we went to enjoy our first drive-in experience, although I think each of us fell asleep from exhaustion at various times during the second feature.

Afterward, my dad drove home triumphantly. But it was a triumph tempered by the realization that metropolitan Washington, DC, like America as a whole, was still far from being integrated, far from being as open as the air to us "coloreds."

Soon, however, integration was to come to DC with a speed that seemed more lightning than deliberate. For example, two decades later an aunt and uncle of mine who had previously lived in the Frederick Douglass Dwellings would buy a house on Brandywine Street in one of those previously all-white communities just above Oxon Run, that street being the same street where one of my best friends—the white boy with whom I'd, in fact, trained for the football team—had lived with his family. When I'd walk home from school with him, walk in the opposite direction from where I lived, my pulse would often quicken through some sense of moving deeper into a white community, a white world. And when I first drove along Brandywine to visit my aunt and uncle in their new home, I passed by my friend's old apartment building knowing not only that his family no longer lived there but that no white families lived anywhere on that street, anywhere for blocks and blocks, palpably sensing how radically Anacostia had changed.

So radically that by the early 1970s practically all whites were gone from Anacostia—as eventually were my family, many of my relatives, and much of the rest of the Black middle-class. That place "across the river" had transformed from an area that in the 1920s had the highest percentage of homeownership in the city and apartment structures of only one half of one percent of its total housing to an area that in 1970 saw 75 percent of itself zoned for apartments.

That transformation came about for a myriad of reasons. But to my mind two are quite foremost: urban renewal and integration.

Congress had two increasingly interconnected problems on its hands between 1930 and 1970 with regard to Washington, DC: the need to accommodate families displaced by the demolition of substandard housing, particularly the alley dwellings in the central city, where many Blacks had lived since just after the Civil War, and the need to expand the federal government, whose size began to balloon during and after World War II.

The National Capital Housing Authority, created by Congress originally as the Alley Dwelling Authority in 1934, was charged with the task of the eradication of alley dwellings and the construction of public housing in DC. Around the same time the federal government decided it wanted to keep its agencies and workers as much as possible near the core of the city rather than push them out to the suburbs as originally planned. That meant condemning housing and acquiring land by eminent domain, particularly southwest of the Capitol, an area that had once been too marshy and mosquito-ridden to be very desirable, an area where some of Washington's notorious slave pens and auction sites were situated before the Civil War, an area that had been allowed to deteriorate into a "slum" by the end of World War II. DC's population was booming, expanding more than predicted after that war, and there were suddenly more low-income families, primarily Blacks, being displaced than there was housing they could afford to rent. In addition, restrictive covenants in the suburbs prevented Black families from leaving the city to find housing, even if it was affordable, which it often wasn't. Meanwhile, height restrictions prevented the government from building true high-rises, either for itself or for low-income families. That is, by law, no building can be constructed in Washington, DC, that exceeds the height of the 555-foot-tall Washington Monument, which when first erected stood as the tallest structure in the world and is at times referred to as the world's tallest free-standing masonry structure, although it's technically not a masonry building at all. Hence, the more sweepingly "horizontal" solution: urban renewal. Or "urban removal," as certain critics cynically say.

Some of my mother's family were "urbanly removed" from time to time over those years, especially from southwest to southeast of the Capitol. And although many of those old row house dwellings in Southwest were like "see-through" houses to me, "shotgun houses," more colloquially—that is, the back doors seemed to lie just behind the front ones—they were nonetheless home to family, and displacement is displacement. When my mom was young, shortly after her father died, she and her mother, sister, and two brothers stayed with relatives in that Black Southwest. And when they had to move, their search for housing was traumatic for her: she was so afraid that they'd wind up homeless and on the streets. Fortunately, they managed to secure the last, demonstration model, garden apartment in a new public housing project near the Navy Yard in Southeast, projects other friends and relatives had moved to, projects that I considered my second home when we traveled across the Anacostia River, with kids constantly running in and out and family packing Mama Davis's four-room, two-story corner place during holiday gatherings, her holding court like the queen of the domain that she was. Especially during the grand New Year's Day celebrations, with joy and happiness, gifts and bowl games, and a feast of chitterlings and pig feet, ham and potato salad, collard greens, sweet potatoes, and of course black-eyed peas for good luck, all capped by grandma's patented three-layer caramel cake with ice cream for dessert. Nevertheless, Mom's early brush with possible homelessness was one "hit-home" example of the fact that DC proper wasn't going to have enough public housing for everyone in need.

But across that river from the central city, from the "real" DC, across that river that met the Washington Channel at Fort McNair and converged with the larger Potomac River at Haines Point, across that river sat an area whose original residents were the Nacotchtank Native Americans (also known as the Nacostines), an area to which there was only the original little 11th Street Bridge for more than a century, an area that didn't get a high school until 1935. Across that river lay Anacostia. All of that acreage, rolling and relatively expansive. Anacostia was suddenly the solution.

And so slowly but surely, as zoning laws changed, public housing projects rose much faster and in greater density in Anacostia than in any other area of the city by far. And slowly but surely the social and economic fabric of Anacostia began to change as well.

Such change was also effected—ironically for some, "tragically" for others—by integration. Gradually, from the late 1950s into the 1960s, with rigid segregation crumbling, middle-class Black families began to leave Anacostia for better, larger homes in other parts of DC and in the suburbs, especially Maryland's Prince George's

County, where the restrictive covenants fell more quickly and the housing was more affordable than in other counties surrounding the nation's capital. Relatives and friends on my father's side of the family began buying lots and having new homes built in P.G. County as early as the mid–1950s. And that American-dream drive to move up and out began to break up the old neighborhood and a certain sense of family, almost literally for me, because for quite some time during segregation at least half a dozen of my relatives lived in homes up and down Shannon Place.

Finally, in 1962, my own family moved as well, from my dad's parents' old house to one we bought in Northeast DC, right on the border between the city and P.G. County—moving to a community whose closest drive-in theater was, unwittingly, the one that had finally welcomed us that night in the 1950s.

Thus was Anacostia "stripped" of much of its Black, middle-class base just as more and more low income Black families were moving into housing projects there. What quickly followed were overcrowded schools, loss of amenities and services, and an increase in rundown housing stock and other kinds of neglect. And neglect inevitably leads to various kinds of frustration and despair. At a time when DC residents were finally getting the theretofore unconstitutional right to self-government, Anacostia was morphing into Ward Eight—the economically depressed voting district that the embattled yet savvy and tenacious Marion Barry (no kin, I'm quite sure, to the original owners of that vast farmland) had consistently championed.

Why, even the Metro subway system built in the 1980s threatened to bypass the area, to go straight from the Federal City to the Maryland suburbs, until finally, under increased political pressure, "low priority" stations were opened in Anacostia, one of them on Howard Road at Shannon Place, just two blocks from our old house.

In effect, a part of DC that in the first half of the twentieth century was benignly neglected, left to its own middle-class, segregated devices, became in the second half of the twentieth century an area to which first too much of the wrong kind of attention and then not nearly enough of the right kind was paid.

Hence, in the 1950s we Negro kids were riding the cusp of an era, blithely unaware of the changes that were in store, our world to a large extent proscribed and circumscribed. And that's one reason why we took our special privileges where we could, namely up on Cedar Hill. For that house on nine acres of land was none other than the venerable Frederick Douglass Home, whose caretaker just happened to be a member of our Bethlehem Baptist church—a church Douglass himself had once visited in its earliest days—and hence favored us more than other kids for prime sledding rights on snowy DC days.

In every season the Douglass home was quite imposing, of course, and it seemed a little strange that to travel up to such a symbol of one of the greatest Black abolitionists and champions of freedom and justice for Black people ever, we had to walk from our all-Black community into a part of Anacostia that was still basically white. But in retrospect one might say that we boys were traveling the great Frederick Douglass's own path, for it was he who in 1877 broke an all-white covenant by buying the house and property from John Van Hook and moving there from the central city.

Two decades earlier, Van Hook, along with his partners in the Union Land Company, had bought up land at the intersection of Nichols Avenue and Good Hope Road and laid out what they called Uniontown. It was to be the first DC suburb, a working class, whites-only settlement (although apparently not for the Irish, who were the "Black" white people of nineteenth-century America) intended primarily to serve Navy Yard workers with lots purchased for three-dollar monthly installments. "Negroes, mulattos, pigs, or soap boiling" was forbidden, something that appealed to those whites fearing the increasing number of free Blacks in their neighborhoods in DC proper. But land speculation, financial panic, and a slowdown in production at the Navy Yard (where my father was working as a machinist nearly a century later) led to hard times for Van Hook and Co. Hence, the sale of his prime, pristine headquarters property to, ironically, one of those hitherto barred "Negroes," albeit a rather famous one.

Douglass died in 1895, but his second wife, Helen, organized the Frederick Douglass Memorial and Historical Association, which was chartered by Congress in 1900. The association and the National Association of Colored Women's Clubs joined forces to open Cedar Hill to the public in 1916. And in 1962 the National Park Service was entrusted with the care of the house. But in the 1950s we boys felt that the gently rolling hill on which the house stood belonged to us on those snowy winter days just as much as Fort Stanton did year-round. We were Black boys dreamily sledding over white snow, pushing through to a time when segregation would give way to integration, and then, little more than a decade later, to one when the population of Anacostia would be just 37 percent white, when the DC school system would be 90 percent Black, when Nichols Avenue would become Martin Luther King, Jr. Avenue, when the Carver Theater would fold and later reinvent itself as the home of the Smithsonian's Anacostia African American History Museum, and then fold again when that museum moved to a new, much larger building up the hill across from Ft. Stanton Park.

Today, Anacostia is overwhelmingly Black and thus "naturally" segregated once again, only this time more insidiously so, for such segregation has a new factor churning within it: social and economic isolation. But much change is in the air—even solidly in the works— as it is everywhere now in DC, it seems. So much so that one current complaint from many Black residents is that their "Chocolate City" is melting in the noonday sun of increased gentrification, with white families buying up property Black families can no longer afford and "moving back in," desiring to be closer to the action again, thoughts of where their young children will eventually attend school placed on the back burner or distinctly on the one marked "private." And what with the Metro so gaily gliding "across the river," property values steadily rising, and new development lining MLK Avenue and beyond, Anacostia is increasingly "in their sights."

Despite all this, however; despite the elaborate plans for all manner of Anacostia riverfront development; despite the creation of a neat though rather circumscribed community of mixed-income townhouses along Alabama Avenue that rests on the site of the demolished Frederick Douglass Dwellings, which had sat on the site of old Stantontown, which was land that had been bought by ex-slave Tobias Henson; despite the grounds of Saint Elizabeths Hospital, the old insane asylum, partially making way for the Department of Homeland Security on its west campus, a sports complex on its east one, and upscale housing and facilities here and there; despite all of that and more—all those so-called manifestations of freedom and progress in this country—I suspect that Black boys sledding down a snow-encrusted Cedar Hill might well still be Black boys reveling in one of the few white realities they feel they can safely touch, embrace, get next to, glimpsed and grasped in the dead of a DC winter. That temperate-climate snow—like integration of any kind, it seems—forever elusive, impermanent, the stuff of dreams.

Pee

I was going to have to pee soon. I could feel it. Feel the tiny little molecules of waste forming inside my bladder, gathering together, collecting themselves, preparing to knock, knock, knock on Urethra's door. Open up, open up, open up, they'd cry, or we'll point-blank back up and flood your head, turn your eyeballs yellow and your brain to smelly mush. Me standing in front of Hart Junior High, its doors now locked because it was late, the long track practice over, everybody gone, and discovering I had neither a token nor money for the bus ride home, meaning I'd have to walk those three long miles uphill and down all the while knowing that I was going to have to pee soon.

And so why in the world didn't I simply pee? Step to the side, into an alley, behind a tree, and pee? Because, you see, it was me. Proper, shy, stoical me. I couldn't just casually open up, come out of the self that hid much of myself in this white neighborhood where I'd been attending school for the past eight months, where I was forever still guarding much of me, the me attached to the natural, sensual "he." For I was a boy with secrets, you see. Or so it so clearly seemed to me. And hence was I bound to get all the way home before allowing myself to pee.

With my schoolbooks and supplies stuffed in my bag I began trudging up the hill, past houses where I knew no one, where I was deathly afraid of simply knocking on a door and asking if I could use the bathroom. In those instances, silence always seemed to be my cover, my protective shield, my way of staving off the world and all manner of embarrassment, real and imagined. Silence, I was good at. It was a way to gingerly assess every situation before deciding—a kind of indirectness, in fact, that my father was famous for.

He rarely answered a question I asked him right away—or if he did, rarely with a yes or no. It's as though he feared commitment, feared being trapped or being wrong. He'd think, mull over, consider for an interminable amount of time, almost begging you to repeat your question, as though he hadn't heard, when of course he had, holding on to it in a kind of passive aggressive way and then at times coming forth with a wishy-washy answer that forced more questions. And thus would the conversation often move: question, pause, question, maybe, question, statement, question, question. Him always having the upper hand, his cards held close to the vest in his silent authority. All that shifting and reticence in a man who was, nonetheless, deeply committed and loyal to family and community, a man who readily, eagerly exposed himself to God, in his prayers at mealtimes and before going to bed, in his attendance at and stirring deaconship in our Baptist church. If only he would have broken through his silences and pauses with me more often, or with my mother or brother or sister, rather than making some active gesture sometime later, assuming that I'd known the answer all along and actually wanted him to do what he'd decided to do, action both delayed and disconnected from direct discourse, and naked feeling.

But then, like father like son. Guarded even as a boy, in control of my demeanor, my voice, my "stirrings." Capable of taking up as little space as possible, of hanging back, pretending to observe when much of what I was doing was trying like hell to keep from *being* observed, from letting some telling part of myself slip up, spill out into the unforgiving open.

Thus did I walk with a kind of dispatch that longed not to call attention to itself. I was in a hurry but didn't want to show it. I couldn't run, although I was fast and in really good shape: too many books and a jiggling bladder that was already beginning to gurgle with incipient doubt. With my stride firm, me leaning into my gait, eyes narrowed, focused, lips sealed against the world, I was determined, come hell or high water—well, not high water under the circumstances—that I would pee at home.

Muffled, controlled, and utterly, or at least seemingly, in charge. Like that one Christmas day when I wouldn't speak.

I was about nine years old, my brother eight, my sister six. We'd dutifully stayed upstairs that morning even though we'd been awake for an hour, waiting with quiet anticipation for our parents to get out of bed, knowing that it was still too early to wake them, for we were sure they'd been up half the night preparing for the day, bringing presents out of hiding and wrapping and arranging them. Or at least *I* was sure, *I* knew they were Santa Claus.

Soon we could stand it no longer. We tiptoed into our parents' room where my brother and sister gently shook them, pleading for them to wake up, me hanging back, already pretending to be above such pleas, already learning to suppress my enthusiasm, to keep my feelings to myself.

My parents teased my brother and sister for their impatience and then made us return to our rooms, my sister right next door to them, my brother and I down the hall farther, past the stairway and the bathroom, to the back room that we shared, I on the top bunk, he on the bottom. Not yet, my mother had said. Things aren't ready yet. Why, I'd thought to myself. What things? What's up? Then my parents got up and into their robes and went downstairs.

My sister sneaked out of her room and sat on the top stair, where she could only see the front door of the house in the tiny vestibule below, not into the living room, which was through an entranceway to the right, no sight of the tree we'd decorated so carefully the night before, having bought it, as usual, on Christmas Eve, when it was drastically on sale, no sign of all the presents we were hoping for. Soon my brother was standing behind her, and I behind him, each of us dressed in our flannel pajamas and robes, each of us waiting, listening, except that for me there was still something up, something else going on, although I didn't breathe a word for I loved keeping secrets, loved knowing, even when I didn't fully know.

Finally, the call from below: "You can come down now." My mother speaking, of course, not my father, the slightly theatrical, mischievous lilt in her voice adding to my suspicions, for my mother loved spectacle and surprise, loved the quirky and the quaint, and above all loved to capture moments for posterity. But the ubiquitous camera was old news. What might be new?

My brother and sister nearly knocked each other over racing down the stairs. I followed coolly, step by cautious step, looking perhaps as prematurely old and leaden as some ill-fated boy in a Thomas Hardy novel.

In the living room my brother and sister shrieked—a bicycle, a new doll, a Lionel train, overstuffed stockings, colorfully wrapped presents. I stood in the doorway observing the scene, watching my father stand back, a wry smile on his face, loving and joyful in his silent way, as my mother snapped away with her camera and more enthusiastically than usual tried to orchestrate the scene. "Look what's over there?" and "What do you think of that?" and "What's that you just opened?" and "Come on, Kermit, what have you got this year?"

I took a step toward a board game I'd asked for. I loved board games, loved the rules and the competition, where I stood a better chance of controlling things through my wits and my need to calculate risk. But then suddenly I stopped when I glimpsed something else: a shiny new machine, half-hidden by the sofa, its thin brown tape winding silently through its silvery mechanisms from plastic reel to plastic reel, winding and winding, making me deliciously dizzy with discovery. My mother was secretly recording all of my brother and sister's spontaneous outcries, and she was longing to record mine as well, hoping to capture every uncensored comment that might insouciantly stumble from my mouth. And that made me more determined than ever to repress my immediate feelings, as though my very soul and the nature of my being depended on it. Hence, like some primitive tribesman who refuses to be photographed, did I remain absolutely silent, continuing to stifle every joy, every surprise, refusing to be coaxed into any verbal reaction, until finally first my father and then my mother knew that I knew and felt compelled to tell my brother and sister, too. They were delighted, happy to have been both tricked and preserved, while I stood triumphant, clever beyond my years, and richly unexposed.

But that sense of cleverness went out the window during my trip to an all–Negro Boys Club camp the next summer, leaving my aversion to exposure to fend for itself. My brother and I had gone for a two-week stay, although we were in separate cabins, housed as they were by age. It was our first sleepaway camp, and I quickly realized that I was going to have a really tough time, because my fellow cabin mates, whose names, faces, and backgrounds I don't remember, all seemed, in short order, to hate me. To them, I was too quiet, too uncool, too standoffish. In turn, of course, they were also "too" to me. Too loud, too silly, too stupid, and too willing to be ... exposed.

The bathroom and showers were in a separate building, and to take a shower everyone would undress in the cabin and walk outside to that building draped only in a towel. And of that ritual I stood in mortal fear. Such exposure, such rank nakedness, which none of the other boys seemed to care about. They'd even prance around back in the cabin in or out of their towels, and even teased each other once, when the counselor wasn't around, about how certain penises poked out, as I turned away embarrassed, hoping to God that mine wouldn't poke out, too.

What is it with me, I wondered? How come I'm so different from everybody else? Not realizing that other boys might also be secretly warring with themselves about all manner of perceived differences.

My trepidation about even venturing into the bathroom seemed to be too much for my body one night during the first week, when it turned against me in my dreams and I woke up to find that I had pooped some in my sleep. It was as though my dreams were the only place I felt free to "let loose." Yet a liberating experience it most definitely was not. I bolted upright in my bunk and quickly got control of my bowels, darting my eyes around in the cool darkness to see if anyone else was awake. No one was, of course. They all seemed to be dreaming peacefully, relaxed, content, secure in their skins, in love with their natural selves.

I stealthily got up, opened my trunk, and took out some clean underpants and pajamas. Then I hurried out of the cabin and to the bathroom, where, starkly alone, I cleaned myself up, put on clean nightclothes, and dumped the soiled ones in a trash can far away from my cabin. No one would ever know about my accident. Nonetheless, from there on it was downhill for me at camp. Too many jellyfish in the water, too much terribly tasteless food, too many sprint races lost to boys I couldn't stand—races I typically won at home. Absolutely nothing seemed to be going right.

The clincher came the evening that each cabin performed original skits for the whole camp. Ours was a stupid little bathroom-humored tale about people riding on a city bus who refuse to sit next to a certain bum because he truly stinks—a detail that the audience was invited to surmise via all manner of exaggerated acting. I remember neither the dialogue nor the story's outcome. But I do remember the fear that I felt having to perform in front of people and the humiliation I felt having been chosen to play the part of the bum.

(Had someone found out about the poop, after all?) What a perfect way to advertise my alienation from the entire cabin.

Of course, I *could* say that my accepting the role of the outsider was an attempt on my part not to be such an actual outsider in the other boys' eyes, an attempt to show them that I could, well, "play along," could be the embodiment of much that all of us feared: being ridiculed, dismissed, rejected. I *could* say that. But it would be a boldface lie. I was bullied, pressured into taking the role. And I felt like crap, which I suppose was the point.

The day after the show I decided that I'd had enough. I called my parents and begged them to come get me. And although I was vague about what was bothering me, they did allow me to come home early, leaving my brother to happily finish the two weeks on his own.

I never returned to that Boys Club camp. Fortunately, by the time I began attending Hart, I *was* beginning to go to week-long Boy Scout camps, this time with a bit more self-confidence and privacy. Nevertheless...

At the top of the hill from my junior high school I walked swiftly past Congress Heights Elementary and onto Nichols Avenue, a main thoroughfare, where I stopped to catch my breath and reassess my situation. At least two miles to go still with a bladder fuller than ever, and there looming across the street from me was a potential savior: a filling station. All I needed to do was walk up to one of the attendants and ask to use the station's bathroom. He certainly would have obliged. After all, this wasn't the Deep South. There wouldn't have been a "whites only" sign on the bathroom door. Sure, it was 1959, and DC was still a segregated Southern town in certain tacit, even de facto ways, but surely a gas station attendant would have taken pity on a desperate though neatly dressed young Negro boy, a student no less, not a "thug." But instead of crossing the street I kept right on walking, as stubborn as hell and still loath to speak. I wasn't going to give in. I was going to continue to exercise my weird sense of self-control and discipline. I was going to pee at home even if it killed me.

Walking and holding it in, walking and trying to not to think about it, walking and wondering who might be watching, guessing by the look on my face the dilemma I was in. Walking through still rather alien territory I normally rode through on the bus, never having to stop, look, or listen much between my house and my school, between my Black community and that white one. Territory I would never have ventured into even by car just a couple of years before, for until recently there hadn't been much shopping for us there, and the Congress Heights movie theater, which I was just passing, had been for whites only.

Keep walking, just keep walking. Don't think, don't feel. Don't desire to be relieved, don't expose yourself for real.

Such fears tended to hound me most of my youth. For example, I was a lousy junior counselor because I was too embarrassed to sit before my campers and lead them in sing-alongs. And I spent practically all of the few dances I went to as a teenager glued to walls or stuck in chairs because I was too shy to ask girls to dance and had no swinging buddies to help me. And believe it or not, when I was ten years old, I actually delivered a heartfelt thank-you speech … to a door. Granted, it was an active door—that is, there were lots of entrances and exits and lots of people, mostly kids, making a good deal of noise on the other side of it. Nonetheless, it *was* a door.

I was in the basement of my church at a youth function one Saturday afternoon. Recently, I'd spent a few days in the hospital recovering from an appendectomy, back when it wasn't an in-and-out-in-a-day-or-so surgery, and while there I'd received lots of get-well cards. My parents had made me write thank-you notes for some and even thank others in person, and since my church youth group

had collectively made me an elaborate card, I made plans to personally thank the entire group that Saturday afternoon. But once I got to
the church, I began having second thoughts. Suddenly, the notion of
speaking before all of them, especially expressing a sentiment, made
me quake with fear. Of course, I had to do it. I'd promised my parents
that I would. But when, and how?

To stall, I pushed through the door from the crowded main
room into the hallway and then went straight into the bathroom.
Not to pee, though. Instead, I just peered and peered into the mirror at myself—at my cowardly, wimpy, reticent little self. How I could
say even a simple "thank you" without showing my feelings, without
crumbling, losing control, without breaking down, crying? For me
that'd be almost close to dying.

And thus did I stare, at times practicing several anemic thank-
you speeches, trying to screw up my courage with every toughening
little squint, as though a reluctant, wooden thank-you would be any
better than none at all.

Finally settling on the shortest if not sweetest statement of gratitude and feeling as brave as I felt I was ever going to feel, I turned
away from the mirror and marched with purpose out of the bathroom. Luckily, no one was in the hallway. Everyone was through the
door I now faced, the din of their activity still as clear as a church
bell. Practice, practice, with my head full of practice, I made a move
toward that door. But then I suddenly froze up once again, for my
heart had begun pounding even more...

I couldn't go through with it. That is, I couldn't go through that
door like that. Yet I also couldn't let down my parents and didn't feel
I could lie to them if they asked about my little speech. I was trapped,
stymied, with only one possible solution, it seemed to me. I stood as
erect as I possibly could and in a soft, shaky voice, nearly a whisper,
I delivered my heartfelt thank-you speech to everyone present ... on
the other side of the closed door. And even then, despite the safety of

distance and "cover," my body was nearly overwhelmed by the words I'd uttered, for in my mind's eye I could see everyone watching me, staring, then moved, then moving, wanting to connect with me further, perhaps even hug me, and such warmth, ironically, chilled me, frightened me.

I shook off those feelings with an involuntary shiver and rejoined my youth group, unaccountably oblivious to the fact that my performance had been a fantasy, or at least fantastical, that no one there would ever know how much I appreciated their get-well sentiments. I didn't understand back then that my pounding heart, sweaty palms, and genuine gratitude were all of a piece, all me, my legitimate feelings, things it was okay to express, to reveal to others, even to the point of tears.

By now, I'd reached the southeastern edge of the loony bin. Saint Elizabeths Hospital, that is. The grounds of DC's famed insane asylum stretched for several blocks, covering more than 300 acres, along both sides of Nichols Avenue (originally called Asylum Road). Shepherded into being by pioneering humanitarian Dorothea Dix and its first superintendent, Charles Henry Nichols, which is why that road became that avenue in 1871, the hospital grounds' high, red-bricked walls and its gates sometimes obscured its buildings from sidewalk view in ways that made walking past it at night a ghostly adventure. I flashed on the notion that St. Es, as we sometimes called it, was perhaps where I belonged, on some ward reserved for weird, neurotic thirteen year olds. But I quickly came to my senses—those at least that I was currently in touch with.

It's a little ironic that that place of confinement and comfort served back then as a sort of demarcation between Black and white communities, the former stopping at the beginning of its northwestern base, the latter beginning at the end of its southeastern one. There was a time, of course, when Saint Elizabeths was far from any community. Established in 1855 as the Government Hospital for the Insane, it was deliberately placed outside of DC proper, south across the Anacostia River up on one of Anacostia's hills. And high on a hill it was, too. So much so that before adequate roads, horse-drawn carriages had to struggle so long and mightily when bringing visitors to see patients that said visitors had to plan on spending the night on the asylum grounds before taking the long trip back down to the river to cross over to the central city. It's said that it was wounded Civil War soldiers who began calling the hospital Saint Elizabeths, after the colonial name of the land, because they were reluctant to admit that they were in an insane asylum. Finally, in 1916, Congress "agreed" and officially changed the name.

Today, of course, the name Nichols Avenue is also changed—to Martin Luther King, Jr. Avenue—now an effortless drive from one Black community to the next, for that essentially is what Congress Heights has become over the years.

Trudge, trudge, trudge down the avenue, now picking up my stride a bit more, trying like hell not to think of the need to pee, knowing that once I passed Saint Elizabeths I'd be more than half-way home. And home was my object. I was going to pee at home. It was now my mantra, a stoic's most precious desire, an ascetic's most basic plea—or simply the warped thinking of a fearful, proper little adult.

Much too proper by half, I suppose. The oldest grandchild on my father's side of the family and the third oldest on my mother's side, with an uncanny knack for being well behaved in all respects, I was a model child. I'd learned that quickly—perhaps a week out of the womb—and carried it with me wherever I went. Teacher's pet, preacher's pet, every friggin' adult's pet. Quiet, studious, independent, and probably in some kids' eyes, dull as dirt, except perhaps when I had an answer they so desperately needed. As I grew older, moved into high school and college, I often longed to bust out, to open up more, but I didn't seem to know quite how, and I think that for the longest time I feared that if I did open up, I would lose my sense of self and simply disappear. Of course, I wasn't a piece of wood. I laughed and cried, cheered and jeered, pouted and sulked and screwed up royally more than a few times. But not often with abandon, not often going on sheer impulse. As I did once, famously, in a classroom.

It was a tenth grade geometry class. The teacher was a squat, bespectacled old woman with a voice somewhere between Julia Child and a scratchy opera aria. I'm sure she knew her subject well—or at least did at one time—but much of that knowledge got lost in the translation, along with the memory and proper pronunciation of some of our names. For example, she continually called a Black girl named Candace, "Cadence." She also no longer seemed to be up to the fine art of classroom control. Hence, she was an honors class's perfect butt, scapegoat, relief from the persistent pressures of accelerated secondary school. Perfect for nearly everyone, that is, except me. Not that I didn't laugh and joke on occasion when the teacher's back was turned. But mostly I tended to empathize with her, feel sorry for her. Until one day when she squinted at me, nearly forgetting my name, and called on me to do a problem on the board.

I went up and immediately saw that the formula was askew. But no matter how hard I tried to explain the error to her, the teacher failed to see it. And because her myopia was causing me to have to linger at the blackboard longer than I wanted to, she became in my eyes nothing but a fat, ugly, useless old woman who didn't have sense enough to see that for months I'd been quietly trying to be on her side—or at least to remain neutral. Finally, out of sheer exasperation at the stupidity of the situation, I threw the chalk across the room. Not at her, just across the room and smack up against a wall with a sharp snap.

For a brief moment, everyone in the classroom just stared at me in stunned silence. No one had ever seen me act so impulsively, not to mention so "improperly." And I wasn't even on the playground. I think that if I'd stayed up at the blackboard a moment longer instead of quickly returning to my seat, the class would have broken into cheers and applause and screamed for me to take a bow. Instead, the teacher cleared her throat, magically saw the error inherent in her posed math problem and apologized to me. She didn't even ask me to pick up the chalk.

In my seat, I practically shook with what was for me a strange kind of exhilaration. It was almost as though this silly, mediocre teacher had deliberately opened a first-floor window and coaxed me into jumping so that I could see I could survive the supposed free fall without dire consequences.

My friends talked about what I'd done for days afterward, giving me mock admonitions about being kicked out of school and brought up on charges of attempted assault with a piece of chalk. But then the talk died down to only an occasional reference to a onetime aberration as I returned to my usual self, safe and sound and in control.

When I passed the last brick of Saint Elizabeths' wall, I was aching to take a piss, even bending over slightly at times to relieve the pressure. And now that I was in a Black community maybe I could more easily knock on the door of a friend. Unfortunately, I didn't precisely know where anyone lived in the apartment complex I was now passing. *My* neighborhood was farther down still, past Birney Elementary and across the bridge over the parkway.

Of course, any Black person, however unknown to me, especially if that person was a woman at home with her kids or grandkids, would certainly have taken me in. But that didn't seem to matter to me. That smiling, loving Black woman would still be a stranger whom I'd have to ask, face-to-face, if I could use the bathroom, which in my twisted logic sounded more and more like something I wasn't supposed to ask, to say, something that would deeply offend her and embarrass me beyond belief.

Nonetheless, as I approached my old school, sitting back and catercorner to the avenue, I suddenly felt the need to return and be comforted—felt, in fact, a sharp desire to go up to the entrance and pound on the front door, plead for some janitor, who must surely still remember me, a former star pupil, to please, please just let me use the toilet. But I didn't. I moved onward. After all, I was no longer that little kid.

Hitting the short concrete bridge at a strong clip now, knowing that once I crossed it I'd be near my church across the street and the drugstore up the way and the movie theater around the bend. And then it would be another half a block, left at the corner store, right at the end of the block, and finally, six houses in, my house, where my bathroom was hopefully unoccupied and awaiting my pee at last, pee at last, thank God Almighty ... or so I thought.

I'm not sure what it was. Perhaps there was something about the swishing of the cars moving back and forth on the parkway under the overpass, something about that sound that served as the last straw. But whatever it was, suddenly, mid-stride on the bridge, Urethra's door gave way, swung open with a mighty burst, and I let loose. I peed. A long, warm, insistent flow of pee down my pants and into my shoes, a pee that stopped me in my tracks and seemed to last an entire week.

I stood stock-still in the middle of the bridge's walkway, my eyes fixed straight ahead. A part of me was so incredibly relieved, and sensually satisfied, as though I were in the gooey middle of one of those scary but wonderful wet dreams I occasionally had. Yet a dream it wasn't, which caused my self-conscious self to wish that the concrete wall on my left that protected pedestrians from the traffic far below were now on my right, protecting me from the cars that passed right by me.

And yet, surprisingly, what I didn't do was panic. My pants were soaked, but more along the inseams than in front, which meant that no one coming toward me, unless they deliberately looked down at my crotch, would notice how wet my pants were. As for anyone behind, I dared not look back. Of course, I could have maneuvered my book bag to cover my front, but that would have made me look incredibly wimpy and only served to call more attention to myself. Instead, all I did from that point on was walk straight home. Well, actually, since my bladder was exquisitely empty, I almost literally flew there, turning toward the end down the alley that came before and ran parallel to my street so that I could enter my house through the back.

Since my parents weren't home yet and my brother and sister were playing out front, I temporarily had the house to myself. I changed out of my wet things and washed them in the sink in the basement. Then I placed them at the bottom of the washing machine and covered them with other dirty clothes, hoping like hell that my mother wouldn't discover them and ask me what happened. Not that I was afraid she would punish me—not physically, anyway. Although it *was* she and not my father who usually meted out that kind of punishment when I was younger, she who would ask me or my brother or sister to get a switch from the yard, she who'd make my heart stop as I stripped to my underwear and awaited the pain from the red welts that would form on my legs after the beating. Yes, it was my bubbly, heart-on-her-sleeve mother who'd do that, not my reserved, stoical father, who mostly punished me with looks of disapproval or, unwittingly, with the cautious infrequency of his hugs and kisses. But no, my mother wouldn't have punished me, I'm quite sure. For my story would have been one about an accident—the result of an exercise in poor judgment perhaps but a rather harmless accident all the same.

It would have been a story that probably would have garnered both a sympathetic hug from her and a place in the annals of her insistent though rather strewn recorded history of our family life. But there still would have been punishment. For having to tell how I came to pee on myself would have caused me a great deal of embarrassment, and being so embarrassed, like being exposed, was to me tantamount to being wrong, which meant to me that I was worthy of being punished and, to fill the void, I would have psychically meted it out myself.

My mother never asked about those wet pants and underwear at the bottom of the washing machine, however. Perhaps she never noticed them in the press of doing the wash. Or if she did, she sensed in her motherly way the story behind the wet clothes and chose to let it pass, the way she let pass my semen-stained pajamas. Private matters, things not to be exposed.

Reading Apprehension

At the start of my senior year in high school I felt on top of the world. I was both an outstanding student and the newly elected president of the student council. I was going to be able to strut around in my new, button-down athletic sweater with Ballou High School stitched in gold on the back and my first name and the letter "B" with a winged foot in its center stitched on the front because I had lettered in track and field the spring before. I had my *own* money in my pocket, thanks to my first, honest-to-goodness, take-taxes-out-of-that-paycheck summer job making all of the $1.21 an hour minimum wage as a busboy in the dining hall of the federal government's Navy Department. And I finally had my driver's license, although I'd gotten it by the skin of my teeth, having bungled parallel parking.

And so there I was on that first day of school, a big-time senior, profiling as best I could, joking and jiving with my fellow honors track friends, when suddenly I felt the urge to mention something that was far, far off last summer's social and vacation scene radar. I announced—practically boasted—that I had read James Joyce's *A Portrait of the Artist as a Young Man* and had really loved it. And without skipping a beat, this ever-cynical, theatrically brooding wiseass, who had never been one of my real friends, rather than launching into a discussion about why I liked that novel so much, dropped his jaw in mock marvel and declared: "You mean you actually read a *whole* book last summer?"

And with that everybody laughed—including me, in a reflexive, defensive sort of way, that is.

Now, under typical teen-guy circumstances that laughter could have easily been interpreted as: who the hell would admit to having read a goddamn book during the summer—especially one that hadn't been assigned? But we weren't your typical teen guys. We were the kind who supposedly read on our own all the time, just like our girl counterparts. Maybe not James Joyce, but certainly something beyond comic books. Hell, how else could we have landed on the honors track "eons" ago when we were little twelve year olds?

But then if reading books and acknowledging it weren't any big deals, what could have been the real impetus for the laughter?

Well, leave it to me in my periodic paranoia to find the answer in the glint I detected in Wiseass's eye. It seemed to say that he was both surprised that I'd managed to read such a book and not surprised that it could well have been the *only* book I'd managed to read all summer. Consequently, he was laughing at the fact that I had tried mightily and essentially failed at being as smart and well-read as he was, or anyone else on the honors track for that matter. And the others' laughing along meant that they all agreed.

And although the laughter was short-lived and we quickly moved on to other, more typical topics—which could have meant, had I given it enough thought, that I was actually the *only* one who'd ever read that Joyce novel—the damage for me had already been done.

Suddenly, I no longer felt on top of the world. For the truth of the matter was that it *did* take me practically all summer to read *Portrait*, which meant that Wiseass somehow understood the depths of a problem I was forever trying to hide: that I was an incredibly slow, plodding reader, that words on the page tended to frustrate me, give me headaches, make me want to sling all manner of books across all manner of rooms, that I had read very few books outside of the ones assigned for school since I'd learned to read in the first grade, and that all of this, despite my academic achievements, made me feel at times extremely vulnerable to Wiseass's kind of discovery and ridicule.

Zip, zip, zip, next page, zip, zip, zip, turn page, zip, turn, zip, turn, book read, done... That's what his comment had brought home to me. All the times I'd surreptitiously watched him and others read: how most of them would zip across the letters, the words, the lines, zip down the pages. How could they do that, I'd marvel. What were they seeing, knowing, remembering so quickly? ... My eyes would spin in my head, making me dizzy with envy. And then I'd turn away in embarrassment. How could they have left me behind like that? Where was I when they were learning to read like that? ... And then, alone, I'd try it myself—try zipping down the pages of some book. But it wouldn't work for me. My head would simply move back and forth as though I were watching a furious game of ping pong, and I'd see nothing but a blur of meaningless words or find myself reading the same words over and over again, until by the end of a page or two I'd see that I remembered practically nothing about what I'd allegedly read. By then my head would be aching and frustration would rumble up from my center, exploding into an often-silent scream as I threw the book across the room...

Now I wasn't so naïve and self-deprecating as to think that everyone in the world was a better reader than I was, if they could, in fact, read at all. What I didn't understand was how someone supposedly so bright could be so disconnected at times from words on the page.

It's only been well into adulthood that I've tried to identify, name, and analyze the main components of my reading difficulties. Or that I've been willing to contemplate the possibility that I was born with some form of dyslexia. For that condition, that supposed "defect," was rarely if ever identified when I was growing up and then later it always conjured up in me images of a child at his desk reversing his letters (discredited as a serious early symptom), of a child struggling with phonetics and spelling, of a child with bad writing skills who did poorly in school. And none of that was the case for me; none of it even defined my primary relationship with words. For I'd always loved language, loved imagery, even loved diagramming sentences. And I'd always liked to write. It was simply that if I wasn't careful, the words as I encountered them on the page would sometimes play tricks on me, or do little interpretive dances, as though they were mischievous little elves. They'd rearrange themselves or some of their letters, or seem to appear and disappear at will, causing me to misread them, which caused me to lose confidence in the veracity of what I was reading, which caused me to have to slow way down when I read, at times vocalizing every word until I'd grow impatient with the whole process and simply stop and move on to some activity I was fully confident I could do. To hell with books, I'd say. I'll find out stuff some other way.

I don't remember the steps of learning to read, or the moment when I "got it." The 1950s Dick and Jane of it all, so to speak. But certainly nothing in that pedagogical process was off kilter enough to cause any alarm in my teachers. I could read. Fine! And I understood what I read. Terrific!

And of course, there were books around our Black middle-class household and education was valued, was quite important. I remember *Rikki-Tikki-Tavi*, for example. I remember my younger brother and sister and I curling up with Mom as she read us the *Little Black Sambo* books—especially her taking great pains to replace "black" with "brown" when she read. For we weren't Black then, we were Negro, although older folks and even my dad still used the term "colored." But clearly we weren't literally "black." No human being was. In addition, Dad liked to read us Uncle Remus stories, with colorful characters like Brer Rabbit and Brer Fox, especially the story about

Fox's Tar-Baby invention. I loved Dad's voices, loved how he acted out the stories, loved the pictures in the books, even the words.

But I don't remember picking up books on my own and reading them. Not even comic books. Much less one of those so-called "children's classics"—the kinds of books some of my friends would later wax nostalgic over, talk about with a combination of excitement and reverence. What I do recall viscerally are books half-read and then tossed aside, a chapter here, a chapter there and then done, or rather undone. In fact, whenever I hear others talk about what voracious readers they were when they were growing up, how they would devour book after book, all that comes to my mind is this unsettling memory of words on the page threatening to devour *me*.

One key component of dyslexia can be having difficulty deciphering and making sense out of non–image-bearing words, words that don't come with pictures the way, for example, "dog," "cat," "table," and "chair" do. Hence, it's actually little, seemingly simple, innocent words such as "to" and "for" and "through" that can throw me off at times. I'll either randomly replace one such word with another, or I'll simply not "see" the word at all. And when those errors begin to compound, they begin to screw up the meaning of phrases and sentences.

Those kinds of mistakes can make reading even short, crisp newspaper headlines, deliberately crafted to be eye-catching, challenging for me at times. For example, "Coup on Tiny African Island" becomes as I read it: "Couple of Tiny African Islands."

When I did begin to read on my own books that I found pleasurable and exciting—*The Hardy Boys* and *Johnny Tremain* and *Treasure Island*, for example—I quickly learned that I required almost absolute quiet in order to be able to concentrate on and absorb the words. Without such ongoing quiet it was practically impossible for me to "get lost" in a book, to become completely absorbed in it. For my ears were continually interfering with my eyes. Overheard words mixing with those on the page, blocking the sense relayed from my eyes to my brain, as though one sense was deliberately rendering another, well ... senseless. And the words on the page would seem to cry out, as if trying to help: "See us, see us, see us without sound. Just the shape of us fixed in your eyes and your brain." But heard words would mass, nonetheless, and snatches of dialogue and disparate stories would mix and merge in my head. And the frustration would come, and then the headache, and finally the slamming closed of the book. Out, out, get me out of this mess! On to the TV or into the backyard, where the words made more sense, or at least didn't hurt my eyes, didn't force that sense receptor to decode them alone.

Another trick my mind can play on me as I read is what I would call "re-sensing." For example, the sentence, "Only recycle designated material," becomes "Only recycle disintegrated material." Or the headline, "Beneath Faults of Foster Care," becomes "Benefits of Foster Care." Or the phrase, "concentrations in fiction and poetry," becomes "concerns in fiction and poetry."

Of course, all of that "re-sensing" does make a kind of sense. That is, my brain is reading for sense, even imaginative, interesting sense. It just happens to be the wrong sense, as though I'm making things up as I read. And the fact that I'm prone to doing that puts me ever on guard, mistrustful of what I see, always needing to go back over to make sure, to at times slow the process down to a dull crawl.

But then if reading was a problem for me, how did I manage to do so well in school? How did I manage to be selected in sixth grade as a member of the first honors class at Hart Junior High School? How did I manage to graduate third in my class at Hart and then first in my class at Ballou? ...

Well, by instinctively compensating, tapping into other strengths and abilities.

First of all, I was very good in math. Concepts, calculations, formulas, and how easily I could decipher and manipulate them kept me working far above grade level in math and science most of the time. Secondly, I was a very hard worker and a stubborn perfectionist, the kind of kid who was determined to do well as a matter of principle, as a way of pleasing both himself and others. And most important, with regard to my contentious relationship with words on the page, I had the wonderful, saving-grace ability to remember them once I'd finally absorbed them—and, along with them, dates, places, facts, and figures. I could *remember* stuff, you see, practically see it in space, even at times in the precise position on the page on which it was written. Not a photographic memory really, not "eidetic," like that of those medieval monks holed up in some castle uncannily copying down whole texts from memory without skipping a beat. But once I truly *saw* something, I could retain it with the kind of tenacity that enabled me to do quite well on multiple choice and true or false tests or on essay questions that asked me to tap into the knowledge and stores of information I'd studied so hard to retain.

It was like a miracle, or at least a revelation. Information, concepts, dates, places, numbers would sit before me in my memory, just waiting to be called up. I would get perfect or near-perfect scores on spelling tests, state capital tests, math tests. I would also speak up in class with answers to questions because the answers seemed simply to materialize in my brain without much effort. And since my reading was slow and plodding, my desire to do well, not to mention my drive to know things, would force me to work through the headaches and frustration because I'd discovered that once I got it, once I understood, I would understand and see for quite some time.

Hence, my grades on those knowledge-based standardized tests in elementary school soared two, three, four rungs above grade level, especially in math, and tended to overcompensate for my less-than-stellar general reading comprehension test scores. Yet even those scores were at least at grade level, for I found that in the absolute quiet of those exam rooms, I could read without undue interference. And because I knew that I was such a slow reader, I would begin by checking out the questions and then searching for key words in the passages to be read, even if I failed to get the gist of everything that was said. Meanwhile, since I was an expert at the rules of grammar, everyone assumed that in all things English I was absolutely fine.

There's also a word recognition glitch in my head that I've labeled "the traveling letter syndrome." In this mode of creative reading, the headline, "Predicting Autism," becomes "Predicting Austin" because the "s" magically travels backward and places itself after the "u" and the "m" morphs into an "n." The phrase "pretty rare now" becomes "pretty raw now" because my eye catches the "w" in "now" and moves it to the previous word to change that word to another—both words non-image-bearing. And "a long checklist of conditions" becomes "a long checklist of donations" because the word "doctor" is in the line above and my brain somehow swaps out the letter "c" for the letter "d," which prompts me to "see" a word that happens not to be there.

But as was my wont with any sign of imperfection in me as a child, I generally kept my reading problems to myself—especially since to the outside world I didn't really have any. And when on occasion I *was* moved to complain, in my rare, rather tentative sort of cry for help, I would usually get one of two reactions.

The most prevalent was that of disbelief.

Come on, you're too smart, too good a student to have a reading problem. Maybe you're just tired. You're studying too hard. Relax your brain, take it easy. Besides, I read kind of slow myself, probably slower than you do.

The other, less frequent response at least took me seriously.

Okay, try to relax more when you read. You don't have to read every word, you know. Especially little words. They're a waste of time. Try reading down the center of the page. Try taking in the words like air, sucking up the sense like drinking through a straw. (Zip, zip, turn, turn.)

And I would nod and nod and then think of President Kennedy and how he could supposedly read something like a zillion words a minute and how people were swearing by those popular Evelyn Wood speed reading courses. And then I would open a book and try and try only to utterly fail. For if I didn't read every word I wouldn't know if I knew. If I didn't read every word I wouldn't see what I saw. If I didn't read every word, they would merely morph into unaspirated letters clinging to the air like ephemeral clouds, only pretending to be the shapes they temporarily seemed.

And then much later, during the summer after my graduation from high school, a valedictorian fearing that my plodding reading might be the end of me in college, I took an unusual speed reading class at a DC YMCA, where the instructor used flash cards with number sequences, gradually increasing both the size of the sequence and the speed with which the cards flashed across the screen. The objective of his approach was to increase my ability to see quickly. And it worked! I did become accomplished at remembering longer and longer number sequences flashing at greater and greater speeds. But then why wouldn't I have? Remembering patterns of numbers was right up my alley. But numbers weren't words, and it was *words* that tripped me up. Words!

But it's the "collapsing letters syndrome" that seems the most insidious. When that problem is in full swing, letters seem to cave into each other as I try to take in the words, which causes my brain to perform some of the oddest misreads I've even seen. For example, once the headline "Man Arrested for Poaching" astoundingly became in my mind: "Many rest in peace." The simple comment in a recipe, "just add water and relax," incomprehensibly became "just wax." And irony of ironies, a phrase on a subway sign that said "chance of reading" did a swirling, headache-inducing dance in my head and instantly became, without my thinking: "clearance."

Maybe it was my dad's fault, I'd sometimes muse. That is, he would sometimes complain about his own reading comprehension problems. How he'd have to say every word out loud. How he'd forget what he'd read by the time he reached the end of a page. How starting to read tended to put him right to sleep. And I believed him, for I often observed him sitting with a book, or even the newspaper, one minute and then nodding right off the very next. It was genetic, perhaps. Although it didn't seem that my younger brother and sister had inherited the trait. They never complained at least, though I never saw them curled up too much with a book, either.

But knowing that Dad and I happened to share the same kind of reading problems didn't comfort me all that much. For it seemed to me that my dad's problems were justifiably connected to a trait of his that I felt I *didn't* have in much abundance: the honest-to-God type-A *doer* trait. As machinist, cab driver, chef, mechanic, builder, gardener, scoutmaster, church deacon, and all-around leader, my dad couldn't stand sitting "idle" for more than a few seconds at a time, it seemed, except perhaps in church or while watching boxing, basketball, or some other favorite sports event. And when he *was* forced to sit still for longer than a second or two, he would characteristically, almost unconsciously, twiddle his thumbs, fingers intertwined and thumbs moving over and over each other, a perpetual motion that somehow seemed to soothe him and keep him connected to his essential self. So why *wouldn't* a book befuddle him, I reasoned? The process of reading wasn't sufficiently active. Unless, that is, the action was about necessary, practical instruction. That is, a book on garden-ing or auto mechanics or tool making, a book that helped explain what he'd already begun to figure out on his own. For he had an uncanny, almost heavenly knack for discovering how things worked, for figuring out how to put complex structures together, for fashion-ing wonderful, well-crafted solutions to everyday problems or even exotic needs, and eagerly soaked up any written words that promised to help bolster his inventive, problem-solving nature, a nature that complemented quite well his "doer" instincts.

But to my mind I had no such instincts. I was none of those active things my dad was. Nor did I suffer from what later was termed ADD. Not that I was a mere carrot or something, of course. I *did* do things; I *was* active. I played outside and rode my bike and danced around to music, at least in my head. But I was principally seen as a little thinker, a budding intellectual, a child who was "smart as a whip," as my paternal grandmother would say. Meaning, of course, "book" smart. A book-smart child with a hidden contentious rela-tionship with books.

Perhaps my problem is that I'm too much in a hurry to know, that I have this kind of itch that leads when I scratch it to what I call "the memory substitute syndrome." For example, I once misread an ad in The New York Times *for a new play. The play was titled, "Anna of the Tropics." But instead I read it as "All in the Timing." That's because the latter title was stored in my memory. Hence, my mind seemed to quickly pick up on only the letters "A" and "T" and then fashion some-thing familiar before my eyes had the chance to relay something new. Perhaps it's nervousness, anxiety, my mind grabbing for something I know for fear that somehow I won't... Perhaps.*

I suppose I shouldn't have taken Wiseass's comment about my possible lack of reading prowess so hard, for all of us in the honors program were about to come up against the mother of all English teachers, Ms. Verna J. Dozier, an always matronly dressed yet essentially elegant Black woman whose twelfth grade class was virtually impossible to get an A in, no matter how many books one had already read or how fast. Only one person got an A that year, I think, and it was neither me nor Wiseass, although I did come close. But despite my relative "failure," I must say that Ms. Dozier had a greater impact on me than perhaps any other teacher in my life, for she gave me one thing that proved to be much more important than an A. It was an even stronger love of words, of language, not only through *her* clear love of them, but also through our thorough analysis of texts and her demand that we periodically memorize and recite in class fine poems and passages from plays, especially Shakespeare's, which made certain phrases and lines and the beauty and meaning of their language even more startling, and hence indelible. And my stronger love fed into a greater interest in books and a more tenacious desire to draw them to me and settle into them despite my frustrations with reading.

It was Ms. Dozier's influence that led me to begin reading more on my own upon graduation from high school, tackling for the first time such daunting novels as Joyce's *Ulysses* and allowing myself to even fall in love with the body of work by an author, reading, however slowly, book after book in succession by the likes of John Updike and Joyce Carol Oates, Dostoyevsky and Faulkner, Conrad and Hardy, Vonnegut and Orwell and Baldwin, Flannery O'Connor and Richard Wright. And I became more and more surrounded by books, more willing to hold on to them, even though I was still certain that engineering and math were my true paths, until I stumbled and tripped up so much on those paths that I was sent screaming wholeheartedly to that of an English major. Not really as a glutton for further punishment, but as someone acknowledging how important the world of ideas through storytelling and language had become to him.

Still and all, true to form, when I took the Graduate Record Exam as a requirement for applying to PhD programs in English, after already having received a master's degree in English and having taken not one math course in several years, my verbal score on that exam lagged behind my math score by a good 100 points.

Sometimes my word confusion even seeps into the act of writing. When I've written things on the board in the classes that I've taught, I've sometimes carelessly written one non-image-bearing word for another—"to" for "for" or "that" for "though," for example—or simply left them out altogether. Or I might substitute one letter for another. Or substitute a word I see and say in my head for some word that's similar in sight and/or sound. "Takes so much" for "thanks so much," for example, with my subsequent embarrassment compounded by the fact that at times I can't "see" the error even when I step back to look because I read "takes" as "thanks." Hence, it often took one of my students to correct me, someone who'd been charged with correcting them, which is why I religiously went over and over again the comments I made on their papers for errors on my part.

And when it's just me, taking notes, working on early drafts, I sometimes "miswrite." For example, scribbling "I hate when this a broken" when I mean and say as I'm writing, "I hate when things are broken." ... Broken, indeed.

When I dropped out of the PhD program at the University of Chicago to study acting at NYU, my reading difficulties weren't uppermost in my mind, although the realization of the sheer number of books I would have had to read to complete my coursework and dissertation certainly struck fear in my heart from time to time. No, it wasn't that at all, for my love of reading was undiminished. Nevertheless...

I reread A Portrait of the Artist as a Young Man *slowly still, reading nearly every word at times, some words more than once, and some misread, which can mar the sense once I've reached the end of a sentence, which forces me to return, frustrated, to the beginning, then forward again, even more slowly this time, wanting to be sure, to be certain that I know. And it's then that I once again ask myself what it all means. Not Joyce, not the beauty of his words and the pleasure of seeing Stephen Dedalus naming his own, finding his way, not Joyce's keen metaphors, phrases, rhythms seeping into my mind, sharpening my sense. No, the meaning, instead, of my continued difficulties with reading, the dyslexic brain-thing of it all. A writer in my own right now, yet one who has such trouble reading still, such trouble keeping certain written words in order. And thus, I sometimes ask, what order can my own writing take? What meaning, what sense can it make?*

Yet still I write, at times scribbling words across the page faster than I can read those that others already have laid, those certified artists, whose work I absorb in book after book, however frustrated with my leaden motion, my at once plodding, at once chaotic eye-scan.

Of course, I could read everything aloud. *For I know that when I do so, when the actor in me savors the words in my mouth, Joyce's art—like that of other artists—often soars on my tongue and in my eyes and my mind. I'd discovered that when I first began performing. This ability to read well when I'm called upon to interpret as I see and then pronounce the words, push them out into the air. Yet I haven't the time really, or the patience or good grace, to read every word of every marvelous book I encounter out loud, piercing the air with meaning that can be so dead to me on the page if I fail to take my time. Still, it's because of time, I suppose, or the seeming lack of it, that I continue to push and push against my "reading apprehension," that I continually return with pleasure to what I might call my own particular "chaos of ardor."*

How I Danced

It didn't take long for me to be at that house party to make me feel diminished, to feel so much younger than everyone else. And not younger than just the girls now either, shooting up and out so much faster than me at eleven, twelve, thirteen years old. But also the guys. Bigger, broader-shouldered. And cooler, too, tougher. Their street language doing a kind of blues dance, heads cocked, eyes cast past things as if they already knew without deigning to look. But then why not me? Didn't I know things, too? And I didn't mean just history and biology and French. I meant all the songs that they knew. *All* of them. My ears just as tuned to the radio, my senses just as keen to the beat. But I guess it didn't matter because all that sense seemed to be stubbornly stuck inside of me, while I hugged the wall and half-smiled into space like some kind of sweet-faced automaton, feeling my body, already sweaty with nervousness and anxiety, seem to melt even further, like that poor, unsuspecting guy in that sci-fi movie *The Incredible Shrinking Man*. Only in my case, to add insult to injury, I also pictured my face growing more babyish by the second as my age uncontrollably counted down. Fifteen, fourteen, thirteen, twelve, eleven, ten, nine ... until I could have passed for everybody's little brother, waiting for his glass of milk rather than whatever spiked punch that seemed to be surreptitiously making the rounds in the dark, low-ceiled basement rec room of this Black middle-class home in DC—the accommodating parents of the host coolly out of sight upstairs. All of which left me only with a preciously pounding sixteen-year-old heart full of unfulfilled desire, rocking and swaying to the music—the pulsing rhythm and blues, doo-wopping, slow-drag pleas alternating with fast-rising Motown gallops, perpetually laced in my sensibility with the Smokey Robinson—falsettoed, hot-breathed wonder of it all.

And yet, to be sure, it wasn't just about height, about not having yet stretched out and up. For I already knew, despite fantasy and wishful thinking, that I was *never* going to be tall and imposing, although I was still holding out for heavy maintenance of what I hoped were the dark and handsome parts, despite awful acne having begun to bedevil me. For neither of my parents was physically very big at all. My dad about five feet eight, a kind of welterweight boxer type in his youth, whose poses in the pictures of him as a teenager displayed the mischievous stance of the cool little con and natural leader of a neighborhood "gang" that he apparently had been. And my mom a mere five feet two, bless her heart, a petite woman with gleaming eyes and a ready smile that, born out of a kind of childhood insecurity, both telegraphed an ardent desire to please and covered a little-girl coyness. And on top of nature's height restriction—although as a burgeoning, brooding teen I would have been loath to admit it—both of my parents were and would always remain in appearance a good ten years younger than their age. That inherited trait embarrassingly brought home later to me when, on a family visit to the university I'd eventually attend, the director of admissions sincerely thought that my *dad* was the potential student, which made me want to grab up a blanket, put my thumb in my mouth, and retreat into a corner like some sullen little Black Linus.

Nor was it that I was necessarily up against the wall alone at that party. For then, as at other times in my adolescent career, there were always those awkward-looking others, those classically nerdy or terminally shy guys occupying some part of the wall near me, although we rarely acknowledged each other, misery most definitely not loving company when said company reminded one of how miserable he must look like to those so matter-of-factly *off* the wall. I even found myself joined by my younger brother Dennis a couple of times, when we'd been invited to a party together. Eighteen months and one school year apart, we were united in our fear of pushy, provocative girls and their chatty, social swirl. United, that is, until Dennis got to junior high school, that all–Black Douglass Junior High I was destined not to attend. Got to junior high and proceeded to step fearlessly into his teens and dance right on past me, more lover boy and party hound now, it seemed to me. Cooler and more suave, more socially adept, with a naturally adventuresome nature and that same mischievous glint in his eye that our dad had when he was young.

It also wasn't as though I hadn't strived to prepare myself for what I was certain would be a crucial test of my hipness. Ever since I'd run into Monica after nearly ten years, and she'd invited me to her birthday party in Northwest DC, I'd been excited about going. She was a girl who'd had a crush on me in first grade. Not that I had dreams of our becoming an "item" again, even though she had the same smooth, coffee-colored skin, fascinating dark eyebrows, and wonderful dimply smile. Hell, we were hardly an item in elementary school, since as a smart, mysteriously quiet six year old I was mystifyingly surrounded by several pretty girls who had crushes on me and innocently, if only for a year or so, just sort of lay back and allowed myself to ricochet among them all.

Nonetheless, I was excited about having been invited by Monica. Excited—and also extremely nervous. For I had never attended what I rightly assumed would be a genuine Black teen house party. Ever since I'd been the only Black boy from Birney Elementary accepted into the DC public school system's new, and nearly all white, honors program at mostly white Hart Junior High, I'd spent my early adolescent years hanging out and doing things with mostly white kids, including going to parties at their houses. Of course, I *had* gone during those three years to the occasional birthday party of one of my cousins and had hung out at some of my brother or sister's celebrations. And there was always music and dancing at the parties my white friends had invited me to. But Monica Conway's sixteenth birthday party in Northwest?! Man, that was going to be "a whole nother thang!"

Which is why, reluctantly, the day before, I'd enlisted help from my hip older cousin Gerald—because I was damned if I was going to ask my younger brother.

Gerald was the oldest grandchild on my mother's side of the family, just as I was the oldest on my father's side. And the only grandchild between us in age was my mother's brother's oldest daughter, Joann, which meant that Gerald and I were the two oldest boys among the cousins. But that didn't make us running buddies, for Gerald was five years older than me and decades ahead in streetwise sophistication and girl-magnet power. A wiry, dashing five feet eleven, he was also one of the most gifted athletes I knew. He ran track, did the forward thing in basketball, played shortstop and pitcher in baseball, and ran and threw from the tailback position on the single-wing-formation Anacostia High School football team, an accomplishment that got him a scholarship to a junior college in California. In fact, he was even good at the board and card games we played, later bringing home from college quickly acquired skills in backgammon and cribbage and chess.

I was in such awe of him at times, although I hadn't shown it much a few years earlier when he stayed with us for a while. For his staying meant that he had to sleep in the bedroom with me and my brother—our younger sister Sheila having her own small room. And there were only bunk beds in our room—me on the top, my brother on the bottom. And I instantly balked at giving him space in my bed, especially since I was bigger than Dennis. Hence, Gerald and Dennis would share the bottom bunk while I slept singly on top. And even with that arrangement, I would sometimes throw inappropriate tantrums at the slightest commandeering of more of "my" space. A real pain in the ass I was for them at times.

Nevertheless, Gerald had graciously agreed to teach his out-of-the-house-party-loop, somewhat nerdy cousin how to swing and sway and dance away—if only perhaps to insure that I didn't sully his own reputation with unspeakable acts of "uncoolness."

Yet the moment he stepped through my bedroom door a part of me balked inside. For in a critical sense of myself, I already *knew* how to dance. Hell, I danced all the time in my head. I had rhythm, dammit. I'd long ago fallen in love with rock 'n' roll and those doo-wop songs Gerald had a hand in introducing me to—he even with a little amateur doo-wop group of his own. Doo-wop by the likes of the Jive Five and the Five Satins, the Crests, the Heartbeats and the Moonglows, the Drifters and the Flamingos, whose "I Only Have Eyes for You" I practically wore out playing. And I especially loved rhythm and blues, particularly those early Motown sounds from Mary Wells, Marvin Gaye, and the Marvelettes, and most particularly the Miracles, with Smokey Robinson's crooning voice sometimes sending chills down my spine and making me feel embarrassingly faint. I couldn't keep that music out of my head. And whenever the pressure of school got to me or I felt isolated and alone and pissed off at the world, I'd call up the music and the lyrics wherever I was, or I'd head for my room and play the 45s I'd begun to collect... And I'd dance, man. Dance on my own. Dance away.

I even created an elaborate, solitary game of DJ, whereby I'd gather any records I had around, stack them in the order of popularity according to my mood, list the song titles on a sheet of paper, and then do a radio countdown show for an imaginary audience. In fact, I even did this before I could afford to buy 45s. I'd use, instead, old 78s I'd borrow from the collections of two of my uncles, records I had to be very careful with because, unlike the little vinyl plastic 45s, those big, beautiful things would break if I dropped them, or even just looked at them hard, it seemed. And then I'd be counting down with the Ink Spots, the Mills Brothers, Nat King Cole, and other artists of my parents' youth, always holding a special, near-the-top position for "I'll Get By (As Long as I Have You)," a version of which I'd heard my dad singing on a recording he'd had pressed and mailed to my mom when he was stationed stateside in the Navy during World War II, which was between their marriage and their having me. So I was in love with all manner of house party music already. And although I wasn't a singer I could carry a tune, especially in my head, could feel the beat coursing through my bones, feel how close to unattainable sex it could make me feel.

And, despite my father's one-time crooning, I'm certain I got that sense of rhythm, that forever music and dance in the bones, not from him but from my mother, who as far as I'm concerned was born to dance. In fact, she probably would have made a better me than me at Monica's party, more gracious and open and willing to let it all hang out. But then I don't just mean dance in the traditional sense, lessons for such she never had anyway, although I'm sure that she would have managed to take them if her musically gifted father hadn't died suddenly of meningitis at the age of thirty-two, leaving her mother to care for four young children during the Depression by working long hours as a housekeeper for several white families. No time or money for dance lessons, although she did see that her own kids at least dabbled in them at a church hall down the street— my sister ballet, me and my brother tap. She cajoled and praised and encouraged us roundly though none of us pursued dance much beyond those weekly sessions and their sweet little culminating recitals.

So not a prima ballerina or a Martha Graham kind of modern dancer was my mother but instead, quite simply, a dancer in life—

dance as a metaphor for her life, her spirit, which danced, moved, strove, whirled anywhere, anytime. If not obviously through her body, her limbs forever poised to move to the beat—even if she didn't know the specific dance, not caring what anybody thought—then through her senses, probing space, checking things out, her eyes ever inquisitive, her ears ever pricked, even her mouth ever ready, insisting on providing whoever happened to be around every last detail of even a routine trip to the grocery store, or willing to sample new tastes, always eating slowly, though, savoring every morsel and then ever willing to sample the courses of others around the table with her at a restaurant. Open, ready, and curious about anything new.

"Dance," her eyes would say, her smile would cajole, "go on, dance, try, *do*." And a real party planner, too—although she was almost always eventually all-night and last-minute about it and consistently relied on Dad for technical support and much of the cooking, with which he was famously expert. And then she would gather and conduct, dish out imaginative party favors and devise and supervise all manner of games, encourage participation, take roll after roll of joyous pictures, and afterward scribble journal notes and thank you notes and notes of encouragement, even if left unsent, since at times they'd seem to scatter and hide among the disparate things she'd gathered, and yet it didn't seem to matter all that much to her, for it was the *act* of creating, recording, acknowledging that was preservation enough.

One summer, when my brother, sister, and I were still at the tail end of elementary school, Mom planned an elaborate Triple-Decker Party Celebration. That is, one separate party for each of us. Friday for me, Saturday for my brother, and Sunday for my sister. Each to be held in our back yard, which was twice as big as most yards on the block because our house was situated on a lot next to an open lot that my parents owned—it having been a wedding present to them from my dad's parents. Hence, our front yard merged with a long side yard into a big backyard. And my mom made wonderful use of the space, putting up homemade outdoor decorations and signs, laying out games and party hats—one of which she always wore herself—and ensuring that music, a separate compilation of our favorite songs for each of us, be piped out from the house: after all, there just had to be dance. And dance we did at each party, each of us having invited our own friends via our own invitations that Mom had us make. Why, not even the rain that Sunday could stop us, or stop my mom. She simply shifted my sister Sheila's party to the paneled basement of my grandparents' house down the street without skipping a beat and danced on from there.

Clearly, she was dancing her way toward being the third-grade classroom teacher she went four straight years to college to become when we were young. Studying steadily and hard, up all night at times, her work spread out before her, almost as a testament to us of what college required, yet what it also could do. Her dance of determination, her drive for further education and possibly a secret vindication after having been an honors kind of student unfairly overlooked in her secondary school years. Pied-pipering along, as much a leader as my dad, coaxing and prodding and romping to the music in her head, letting it spill out freely and generously, ever optimistic that everyone could, and should, be open to the spontaneous dance of everyday life.

And I'd inherited that spirit; I'd swear I had. It was simply that I didn't always know how to show that I had, and how to connect it up with social and physical contact the way my mother could. The spirit of my mom trapped in the reserved, unduly self-effacing body of my dad. A yin-yang kind of thing, I guess—or at least one hell of a push-pull mess.

Gerald was having none of that though, particularly since I didn't tell him any of it. At least not right away. What he saw before him was a sixteen-year-old Black boy who seemed not only out of touch with his body but afraid of it. Hence, did he proceed to show me the latest dances, the hippest stances. And as the music churned and my cousin coached, I did begin to relax some out of my embarrassment. Yeah, the groove was working, things were happening. After all, I wasn't a damn klutz, I was just nervous and scared and perhaps more than a little young for my age.

But then, suddenly, in the middle of some James Brown screech, it began to cross my mind that in a way my cousin—granted, at my request—was trying to teach me how to be something I already was: a Black teenager. Or was he simply trying to teach me to be a *groovy* teenager? Or a *hipper* Black person? And if any of the above, what the hell had I become during my years of junior high school, my years of "hanging with white kids?" Some staid old white guy?

Yet that was too simple, too much of a cliché. Black kids with natural rhythm, white kids without any, and thus Black kids without any being pale versions of themselves—in a creepily warped sort of syllogistic way. It seemed like some silly Amos and Andy sitcom episode in the making. And that's when I think I said: "Stop. This is dumb. I already know how to do this." And my cousin retorted something like: "If you think this is dumb, then it doesn't matter if you 'know' how to do it." Apropos, even if off my meaning. And hence did I continue to persevere, brushing up further on some steps, some moves.

Afterward, I thanked my cousin for his time. He said: "No problem. You'll be fine. Just relax and have fun. The dance'll come."

Dance ... yeah.

And by dance I also mean stance and style, fashion and profile. The dip and sway of one's body to some inner beat, some inherited pull perhaps, some cultural spirit, one's whatever roots. Also, that sense of worldliness and pleasure, which I'd sometimes associated with experience, which meant the opposite of innocence and was, naïvely for me when I was even younger, in inverse proportion to how much time one spent in church.

I'd latched on to that concept when I met Earl, a friend of my cousin Joann, when I was eleven or twelve, and to my true delight found that I had come face to face with a Black boy who, although older than me by a couple of years, was younger-seeming, meaning less cool, less hip, less worldly. And the fact that Earl was a staunch member of Joann's family's Holiness church and spent much of his time there, much more by far than my Sundays at my Baptist church, caused me to put two and two together as I struggled to latch on to any strategic social advantage in the pubescent wars. Hell, Earl could have been my younger brother, and his joking around with me and Joann at her house confirmed it. He danced the dance of a kid brother, talked the talk of one, too. He seemed so soft—not in any effeminate way. Just "unschooled." Joann noticed it, too. We talked about it, laughed about it when he went home, made prissy rhymes with his name. It sort of made me a closet bully. And for me that was cool. *I* was cool, cooler than I'd ever been, it seemed. Cooler than Earl, anyway.

My churchgoing vs. worldliness theory even got a boost *in* my church, Bethlehem Baptist, when I was asked to serve on the junior usher board, which ushered during the Sunday eleven o'clock service about once a month. Eager to be ever at the ready during the entire two-hour service, I soon learned from the senior, more experienced junior ushers that it was much hipper to serve only when absolutely necessary, which meant as the congregation was entering, during collection time after the sermon, and as the congregation was exiting. As for the sermon itself, forget it. Once our minister got up to preach, the older junior ushers quietly headed for the church door, pulling me and other newbies right along with them, past Black-owned Mason's Funeral Home, which always seemed to me to be both too conveniently located and too close for comfort, and across Nichols Avenue to the Black-owned Anacostia Pharmacy. Safely in "Doc Qualls's" establishment with our white gloves stuffed in our pockets, we could hang out on stools at the soda fountain eating ice cream and drinking cherry cokes until the sermon was over and the hymnal calling for new members to come forward began.

One thing that fascinated me about this somewhat sacrilegious routine, apart from its sheer ballsiness, was how quickly the guys shook off their dutiful usher demeanor and danced this hip dance of the street as they crossed it, a dance I was unsuccessful in copying, mostly from fear of being caught. But it was clear that these guys were no Earls. There wasn't nearly enough religion in them for that.

Another thing that wowed me was the guy behind the soda fountain. His name, appropriately, was Freeman, he was probably in his early thirties, and he was as cool as could be. Jerking those sodas with aplomb and telling tales, with a wicked upturned smile, a Clark Gable mustache, and Jackie Wilson processed hair, Freeman was the epitome of style to me. I half expected him any minute to leap onto the counter and break out in a rendition of "Lonely Teardrops." And what further fueled my half-baked theory was that as far as I knew, Freeman *never* went to church. Or at least he sure wasn't at any of the Sunday services we ushers attended to.

And as we coolly headed back across the street, my fearless leaders having uncannily anticipated the Sunday sermon's end, I felt as wicked as Freeman's smile, my body infused with a rhythm and style that good ole Earl seemed to lack, a very good thing since I could still have been placed on the path to Earldom if it hadn't been for an irrevocable rift in the church membership.

The rift was over money and leadership decisions, I think, and led to our dynamic, well-dressed pastor, after only a couple of years on the job, leaving to establish a church in Northeast and taking a portion of the Bethlehem congregation with him, including some members of my own extended family, although not us. Thus did I survive that pastor's proposal to me, eleven years old and an upstanding new church member, whose demeanor and intelligence led some to look upon me as a pastor in the making, although for the life of me I couldn't see why others couldn't see my lack of ministerial fire under my cloak of righteousness, which to me was also a sham. And his proposal? That I be the first youth assistant to the pastor, sort of like a glorified altar boy, with absolutely none of the current altar boy/church leader suspicions.

My duties were still rather inchoate, but some would have been being close at hand at least every Sunday, writing for the church newsletter, and making certain announcements before the congregation. But I blew the announcing part on my very first try when I stumbled one Sunday over a little piece my deacon dad helped me prepare that included verses from the Bible, a text I frankly had no interest in studying beyond my typically facile memorization of the names of books (in exact order) and people and places for Sunday school. For me that public embarrassment would have been enough to cause our pastor to alter my status as "first altar boy." Yet I could still picture myself being led by the nose into and beyond Earldom like a good little boy had not that pastor gotten too big for himself and the church brought in a less imperial young man of the cloth. And thus did I become perhaps the only member of Bethlehem Baptist to have been "saved" twice—my body spared, again according to my theory, the kind of uncool stance that would have made my teenage years even more socially contentious.

Nevertheless, dance, Kermit, dance. White kids, and their white parents and chaperones, looking to me to be a dancer, a performer, someone with natural rhythm, which made me feel gawked at whenever I was out on the dance floor among them, because although I *could* dance well enough for them, and I *did* have "natural" rhythm, I didn't think it had anything to do with my being Black, which seemed to be at the core of their wonder. It was as though I was being perceived as some kind of one-man minstrel show, a Black boy in black face. Yet I also knew that they meant well, that they were even genuine in their connections with me and their ephemeral deep friendships. It's just that when I stepped outside of myself and watched my own performance, looked at how I danced, I felt like a smiling, willing representative, perhaps the only Black kid everyone could say that they knew, could measure their picture of Black boys by, the picture they had of them in their heads, or in their drive-by viewings. And then I'd want my observer self to stop my dancing self. To freeze the dance and give a lecture. To "break bad" in some other way.

But I also remember times when I flatly didn't dance. Couldn't dance. Especially early on. Too shy, too alone as a Black boy among them—the white girls hovering or staring, the white boys daring. What will he do? Who will he choose? Who *can* he choose? And yet: "Go on, Kermit, dance. We know you can. Go on, let's see. You love who we love: the Everly Brothers, the Crickets, the Diamonds, the Coasters, Buddy Holly, Paul Anka, Chuck Berry."

And then gradually, in fits and starts, I learned the power of being the one and only, the power of how, even as others grooved to the beat, they at times looked to me for some rules of the dance they didn't yet know, for ways of better moving they thought I might show. "Go on, Kermit, dance!"

So then why hold back at Monica's party? What the hell was going on?

Well, first of all, besides Monica, I didn't know anyone there. A Black teen among Black teen strangers. A different neighborhood, different world. And since I only had Mom's *love* of the dance, not her instant way of displaying it, of insinuating herself, of doing the social dance that must most often accompany that literal one, I was stupidly stuck, despite Gerald's echoing voice. "Relax, have fun. The dance will come, come, come...."

But a more important reason was that, unlike my little junior high dances, this house party was full of Black kids. Nothing but

Black kids. I was only one among many of my own and suddenly feeling not quite sure that I *was* one or that they *were* my own. There at Monica's, Blackness was a given defined by the many. And to my eyes those many, those confident Black teen strangers, those experts in the dance, seemed to be *daring* me to dance—dance before and among them, dance the dance of Blackness, show them the moves, the grooves, the rhythms, prove to them that I was truly who I was perhaps only pretending to be.

Oh, the ever-pounding pulse of my persistent paranoia. Which stopped my feet. But also kept me off voice. For the voice is another way that one dances, the rhythm of language and talk, the play of lips, larynx, and tongue, waves on air that also make a plea for self-definition. The voice has its own style and color and tone: soft-spoken or loud, squeaky or smooth, tentative or self-assured. And the words we choose and how we pronounce them, the accented idiom of it all, the call and response nature of our mode, can distinguish us by— or saddle us with—a cliché, just as much as body movement and our ability and willingness to express it can.

So perhaps then my failure to show how I could dance was stopped by my fear of the dance of my voice, its sound patterns and idioms, its odd accent, how it had already begun to "evolve" into that which hasn't left me to this day, that "funny-you-don't-sound-Black" sort of vocal dance, akin to the "you talk proper" or "you talk so well" sorts of compliments, which can be much more disorienting to the person whose ears have been privy to that vocal dance, to my voice's unintended ability to "pass," without being privy to me in person.

Such as the time when I was living in Wichita Falls, Texas, stationed in the Air Force there after college and just beginning to act and work backstage in a community theater when I cheerfully gave some current production information to a white woman over the telephone only to have her thank me and then incidentally want to confirm that the theater wasn't too near "Niggertown." Clearly, she thought she'd been casually conversing with a white man. Or another time, still in the Air Force in Texas, when two white fellow officers and I supplied voices in a script that had two white and one Black airmen as characters, only to have the base commander roundly reject the completed tape because he'd wanted one of those airmen to be Black, and dammit, one of those airman was going to have to be *Black*.

(Such errors also occur, sight unseen, between Black people, by the way. Or even quite seen, as when the preschool daughter of a cousin of mine, who was growing up in DC, turned to my talkative preschool niece, the daughter of my sister, who was growing up in suburban Virginia, and very frankly and innocently declared: "You talk funny.")

Or, to merge the play of body and voice into one unified defining dance, when I, as a member of the Second Company of the Williamstown Theatre Festival in Williamstown, Massachusetts, complained to my all-white company members—which included such fine, future successes as Jamey Sheridan, Amanda Plummer, Betsy Aidem, and Brian Benben—about the lack of definably Black roles in the plays we were doing, a brash, talented, street-wise young white actor retorted in dead seriousness: "Why? You're not Black. Shit, *I'm* Blacker than you." Which, after a theatrical pause, made everyone laugh—including me. Although it was no joking matter. In fact, it was even more serious than a Freudian slip. For what that actor meant was that his background and attitude and natural demeanor qualified him more as a Black man than mine did me. Hence, according to him, I was *always* acting—on stage in whatever role I'd been given and offstage as a kind of wimpy white man. And later, when the artistic director of the company offered to do a reading of my first play, which included a white man, a white woman, and a Black man, and I asked that young actor to read the role of the Black man so that I could sit back and hear my play—hear, in effect, how the characters danced—he enthusiastically agreed. Ironically, though—and unfortunately for him—since the Black man in my play was more like me than the white actor as a Black man, the actor couldn't play "Black"—that is, not as Black as he believed that I wasn't.

Dance, anyone? ...

But in the final analysis that fear of not sounding Black enough couldn't have been a factor in my not introducing myself to others at Monica's party because I was yet to be aware of what my voice sounded like to others, of the way perhaps my voice might have seemed to dance away from the way I ostensibly looked.

No, my failure to dance at that house party was all mine, all in my person, my personality, all in who I was at that discrete moment in time. In other words, I failed to dance because although I was my mother's son, I was clearly *not* my mother. And watching Monica cling persistently to a guy who looked to be a seasoned high school senior, as many of the other guys did, didn't help much, either. In the dark yet illuminating milieu of that party, I felt I'd become to Monica merely an old first grade crush turned curiosity now (*how're you doing, having a good time? Sure...*), a bauble from her past who—uncool of uncools as far as public boyfriends went on one's sixteenth birthday—was still pretty much the same height that she was!

Of course, there were other parties. Most notably the eighteenth birthday party my parents gave for me—pulled off with the help of my brother and sister and my Ballou High School classmates, who traveled from Anacostia to Northeast DC where my family had moved, strategically parked their cars, and squeezed themselves into our little basement rec room so they could scream "surprise" at me and send shivers down my spine. My white friends, the ones I'd danced through secondary school with, excited about being able to pull something over on someone who, rightly or wrongly, had such a reputation for knowing. Yes, my white friends, and a spattering of

Black friends from the past, although not Monica and her whomever boyfriend. This was *my* party, after all—with music, to be sure, but practically no dancing, as I recall. In fact, it took the rest of adolescence for me to feel comfortable dancing at parties without caring what others might be thinking about me. Just as it's taken me a lifetime, and still counting, to be fully comfortable with the totality of my dance of self.

Fire

Summer days—and sometimes nights—in Washington, DC, tend to be hot and humid. Not real Southern-city hot and humid, though DC *is* below the Mason-Dixon line. It was built on swampy land chosen by George Washington and donated by Virginia and Maryland, and Southern, often cracker Senators maliciously kept a stranglehold on her economy for nearly a century and a half. Now still, some would say.

But DC gets hot and humid enough in the summer. And without air conditioning, which my family didn't have when we lived in Anacostia, the heat meant that we kids had a good deal of sprinkler time in the backyard and lots of trips the short distance to Fairlawn Park to go swimming, once the pool was integrated, or to catch the breeze coming off the Anacostia River; and much practiced pleading with our parents when the ice cream truck stopped on Shannon Place; and many a cheap, patented Frazier "snow ball," which we made by freezing concentrated, sugared Kool-Aid in plastic cups just long enough to produce with a few jabs of a fork a delicious icy slush. We'd also play softball in the broad, L-shaped alley behind some of the Shannon Place and Chicago Street homes or down the street in the schoolyard of old Birney Elementary, where my dad went to school and where I went for kindergarten; or we'd ride our scooters and bicycles up and down the sidewalks; or on Saturdays put together 20 cents each for children's tickets (adults' were 35 cents) to the Carver

Theater just around the corner so that we could spend most of the morning and afternoon watching cowboy serials, cartoons, newsreels, and hopefully a double feature of horror movies. All of which helped to make the summer heat an afterthought.

That was the kind of summer day it was promising to be when my mother and I, home alone as she prepared breakfast, heard the siren sounds of fire engines drawing closer and closer until they screeched to a stop nearby. I raced to the front door to look out and saw smoke billowing and neighbors hurrying around the corner on Chicago Street, half a block away. More excited than fearful, I yelled to Mom, "there's a fire down the street," and took off out the door. My mother quickly followed.

When we rounded the corner down the block, we saw firefighters already beginning to bring under control a fire on the second floor of a row house, a fire that was visibly more smoke than flames. Unfortunately, they were also carrying out on a stretcher a young man who, according to the buzz, had been badly burned. He was someone in a family most of us knew, and everyone around me was upset, some crying, others wondering about the safety of the adjacent homes. Someone speculated that the man had been smoking in bed, as if to both provide a reason for the tragedy and assure everyone that it couldn't happen to either nonsmokers or more careful folk. Another whispered a "thank God no one else was hurt," especially the young children who lived there. But through all that collective assessment I simply stared with a strange sense of detachment at the charred exterior of the second floor, smoke still seeping out, water from the fire hoses dripping down—stared with one thought paramount in my mind: that I had missed seeing the shooting flames.

Perhaps mistaking my silence for mild shock, my mother comforted me as we headed back. But when we reached our front yard we were caught off guard and momentarily disoriented by the smell of smoke once again and then realized that it was coming from our own house. We rushed through the gate, up the front porch, and through the front door.

Inside, smoke from the kitchen was beginning to curl into the hallway. My mother said something like, "Oh, my Lord!" Then we raced down the hall to the kitchen where smoke was pouring from the electric oven. My mother gulped and pulled down the oven door, revealing a long pan full of burning bacon and grease.

In an instant I was overtaken by pounding, heart-stopping fear, which stiffened my body. Suddenly, the flames I had regretted not seeing down the street were staring me right in the face.

And I began to panic. What should we do? Try and put it out? With what? Water, rags? Should we run? Call the fire department? ... All of these questions and more racing through my mind in a split second.

Meanwhile, my mother went into action. With no fire extinguisher around, she grabbed up two potholders and yelled that she was going to try to get the burning pan out of the oven and across the kitchen to the window, which looked out both on our side yard and onto the cement stairs that led down to the basement. Her thought, I suppose, was to get the pan out of the house rather than try to drop it into the kitchen sink where the flames might spread to the cabinets before she could douse them. But the window screen was down and there were curtains on the window. What about that, about them? Shouldn't I rush over and punch out the screen and rip down the curtains? I didn't know, didn't ask, didn't do anything. I was too petrified.

Before I knew it my mother had dropped the potholders and raised the screen. Then, she took up the potholders again and bent down to take up the burning pan. And that's when I began yelling at her that she shouldn't do it, that she'd get hurt, that the fire was going to spread and the house burn down, that we should call the fire department. But she just kept saying that there wasn't time, there wasn't time. She reached into the oven, as I continued to shake and stupidly wonder where the fire engines were, why I didn't hear their sirens, why they weren't coming to help.

And thus did I just stand by and watch my mother take that burning pan out of the oven, maneuver it to the window, and throw it out, miraculously avoiding setting the curtains or anything else on fire. We then rushed out the back door, where Mom took up the garden hose and doused the flames, which had already begun to dissipate on those cement basement stairs.

Later, after we'd opened lots of windows to clear the smoke from the house, and Mom began tending to a couple of tiny burns on her arms, I broke down crying. I apologized for not helping her, for being so scared, for not being brave enough to do anything. She held me and told me that it was okay, that things worked out okay. Besides, it was her fault for rushing out of the house when she knew that she had food in the oven. That was the lesson learned. And although I, too, had known that she'd been broiling bacon and could have reminded her of that fact, I allowed her to take all the blame, even as I thought of the flames shooting up and how brave she had been in the face of them.

It was a jarring moment. For the first time in my life that I could viscerally recall, I'd been afraid of fire. But that fear apparently wasn't yet strong enough, for later that summer we had another fire, literally in our own backyard—a fire that scared me for a different reason.

It began one evening with my mom rushing into the kitchen from our screened back porch to yell at my dad that the shed was on fire. Dad and my brother, sister, and I hurried out back with Mom and gasped at the flames shooting up from the wooden shed that was about 50 feet from the house, right at the edge of the back alley, which are so common between streets in DC. And I do mean flames shooting up, not just smoke.

Dad went to the phone to call the fire department, but someone else apparently already had because we heard sirens sounding and horns blasting. Hence, the fire trucks seemed to arrive almost instantly, but not soon enough to save our shed, which had gone up like a tinder box because it was an old wooden structure, about 12 by 15 by 10 feet high, a place where my parents stored old wood and half-discarded items and where we kids sometimes played spooky games of hide-and-seek, ever vigilant about stepping on protruding nails.

As folks gathered around yet another neighborhood fire, my family sadly watched our shed burn down. Every one of us, that is, except me. Not even when my mother tried to coax me into observing how the firefighters did their job did I agree to watch. Not as a result of my kitchen fire experience, however. I didn't watch because I knew that the fire was my fault, and I was hoping that I wouldn't be discovered, that I wouldn't have to confess, that I could somehow just disappear.

When my dad called me to come out into the backyard as the firefighters were putting their equipment away, I knew I was in deep trouble. Standing with him was a white fireman, tall enough to loom over both me and my dad. He'd been talking to my dad about the possible causes of the fire and my dad had revealed that he had seen me and a friend playing outside near the shed earlier that evening. Dad asked me what we had been doing. I looked at him, then at the fireman dressed in what seemed like a ton of thick protective clothing, then down at the ground. Nothing, I mumbled. Just playing.

I didn't want to say any more, but I had to say more. They were waiting for the rest. After a moment, I finally confessed that my friend and I had been fooling around with matches, lighting sticks, when some of the grass near the shed had caught fire. But we'd quickly stomped it out and left. We stomped it out, I swore. And the fireman simply replied that the fire probably hadn't been completely out, that it had probably smoldered for an hour or so, and then rekindled all of a sudden. Hot day, dry grass, old wooden shed, flash fire.

By now I was too embarrassed and ashamed to look at either the fireman or my dad. I felt like a clueless four year old instead of the ten year old I think I was that summer. At the same time my mind focused strongly on one provocative-sounding word: smoldering. I sensed what it meant. The fire had been sort of snoozing, lying in wait, hiding in the grass, biding its time until the right moment to flare up, bursting into red hot flames when it could stand out against the near dark, when I, when everyone, could see it fully, roaring mightily enough to taunt me, laugh at me, get me in trouble.

Lost in those thoughts and filled with remorse, I heard practically nothing else that fireman said to either me or my dad. The next thing I knew, he and his fellows were gone and my brother and sister were peeking out of the back porch window at me and Dad, who was clearly angry with me, but showing it in his usual controlled, almost reasoned way.

Frankly, I don't remember what my punishment was. It certainly wasn't traumatic: my parents didn't mete out those kinds of punishments. Our shed and its ragtag contents were gone. And that was a loss. But they were thankful that no one had gotten hurt—just as no one had with the kitchen fire. But for me there was a just-as-important "just as": once again I had failed, failed to extinguish a fire.

Thus began my slide into more than a year of the fear of fire, fear of its control over me, which was manifested most vividly in my dreams—dreams of flames shooting up, of being trapped in burning buildings, of seeing loved ones hurt, of feeling fire on my flesh. Bad, bad dreams. But not nightmares in the sense of my waking up screaming or crying, my sheets soaked in sweat. My fear, like many of my reactions to things in my life, was more of the, well, *smoldering* kind, with only intermittent, sudden, at times inappropriate outbursts. Generally, I kept my fears and my dreams to myself, keeping them bottled up inside, suffering in silence, perhaps as my way of punishing myself, while during my waking hours, although not absolutely eschewing fire, being very wary of it, wary, that is, until I was mercifully released from much of that fear by coming to the rescue of my very own tree.

A present from my parents for my twelfth birthday, my tree was a maple sapling not even as tall as I was. I'd seen it in a tree nursery we had visited in the area and thought it would be cool to transplant and nurture a tree and watch it grow. And I loved watching and tending to it, too—not that my tree needed much tending to until it needed my protection.

This third fire, like the second, also started in the grass, but this time it wasn't my fault: it was our neighbor's. To us kids she was an old, eccentric, sometimes crabby woman whose windows on the side of her house that faced our yard we'd managed to break more than once with errant baseballs. Nevertheless, we put up with and stood by each other well enough. It was just that kind of neighborhood. It was also a time when it was still legal to burn your trash in big metal drums in your backyard. We certainly did so. Yet when our neighbor's trash-burning got out of hand one afternoon and sent wayward sparks flying into her grass and spreading fire along and under the chain-link fence between our yards, she made me see red.

My family had been inside when the fire first began licking at the base of my treasured maple tree. By the time we'd been alerted and had gotten outside, our neighbor was beginning to stem the grass fire in her yard, but my tree was in deep trouble. I cried out, but I didn't freeze, nor did I retreat: I leaped into action. With my family's help, I connected and dragged the garden hose to my tree and watered all around it and up and down the fence. Between us and our neighbor we were able to put out the fire, making sure that nothing was left smoldering in the grass. My tree was singed but still standing, as it would for some time to come, and I seemed to have turned a corner in dealing with my fear of fire. In fact, my relationship to it was destined to deepen and grow more complex.

It began perhaps when I was in my mid-teens. That's when I first observed my paternal grandfather, who had lived in our old house with his family when it was *his* old house, staring silently into the flaming-hot furnace coals in the back utility room of the basement of his second house, which was a block away from us on Shannon Place. When I glimpsed him, only briefly yet quite vividly, without disturbing him, I wondered what relationship he had to those flames, to that red-hot heat, what mysteries lay behind his stare. What was he trying so hard to see, to figure out, to come to grips with? What was it in that furnace fire that drew him like a moth to the flame?

It was rather disconcerting to watch him that way, yet also alluring, captivating—red hot and dangerous. The kind of danger I perceived whenever I was asked to go down to the basement in our house and "light the tank," which we often kept off to conserve energy when we were away, light it by opening the metal door to the cylinder contraption, striking a kitchen match, turning the oblong metal knob that allowed the gas to flow, and placing the lighted match to the gas, the flames curling up to heat the tank's water. Anticipating the swoosh of the flames often filled me with anxiety even as I descended the stairs with the book of matches, yet once the flames were engaged I was fascinated by the sense of unleashed power and would myself stare for a brief time, although the flame's metaphor wasn't in me yet the way it appeared to be with my grandfather.

My grandmother, who had been an occasional seamstress and dressmaker for congressmen's wives and had retired from the Government Printing Office just as her husband had, told me that Grandpa could stare for hours at that furnace fire. And when he wasn't in the basement he was up in his bedroom in nearly total, self-imposed isolation—only coming down to eat, but rarely leaving the house, her dutifully caring for him that way for the last ten years of his life, missing all the retirement trips she'd once looked forward to their going on.

And when I would visit my grandfather alone in his bedroom,

as other relatives faithfully did, my teenage and then young adult self, remembering how quietly vibrant he used to be, would begin to focus particularly on his eyes for vestiges of that vibrancy, as gradually, after a quick smile followed by an awkward silence, he would get around to asking me the question he almost always asked, softly, tenderly, and with deep sincerity: "How much do you weigh?"

The first couple of times he asked me that, it struck me as an odd, off-putting, perhaps even trick question. But my statistical answer would elicit nothing much more than a nod from him: the question was never a set-up for any larger discussion. Eventually, though, when asked, I began to interpret that question differently. It became for me his clear, clean, genuine way of charting progress in his oldest grandson without the burden of trying to digest potentially disorienting details. And then his eyes began to reflect to me, even in their sadness and almost involuntary opaqueness, a smoldering kind of intensity inexplicably trapped inside. It was an affect that in some ways I'd one day come to recognize in myself, on a much less crippling level, of course. Recognize it through insight not only in the mirror, but also upon reflection in many of those pictures of me as a child, rarely smiling, or if so, rarely with a full-out, teeth-showing grin. Such a serious-looking young man I often seemed to be.

And now when I think of my own struggle with depression, I sometimes think of a smoldering fire and of grandpa's eyes. I picture a tiny furnace in both our heads fueled by a whimsical combination of chemistry and psyche and heredity, and I wonder if there was some discrete moment in my youth—as perhaps there was in his—when the first embers began to shape themselves, undetected, threatening to flare up when conditions were ripe into an energy-consuming fire that I sometimes fear I'll never be able to fully extinguish or control.

Of Crickets and Boys

I

"Grab him," my brother urged. "Quick, grab him."

I hesitated, my hands shaking.

"Go on," my cousin said, nudging me. "Just reach down."

Just reach down, all right. To me there was no "just" about it. Nonetheless, I stretched out my arm tentatively. In doing so, however, I nearly lost my balance, my right foot scraping the ground, which alerted the cricket and caused him to hop and disappear under a raised portion of a fat tree root.

My brother sucked on his teeth. "You're too slow," he said.

"It's okay," my cousin assured me. "We'll find another one."

Soothing words. Except I didn't *want* to be soothed that way. I didn't *want* to find another one. I didn't *want* to hunt for crickets—turtle or no turtle.

We were under the apple tree in our backyard. A huge old tree that produced tons of green cooking apples in the cool of October. But this wasn't October; this was a typical hot, sticky day in July, a day that for me was getting hotter and stickier by the minute.

"I hate those things," I whined.

"They're just bugs," my brother said with a superior shrug of his shoulders. He relished the fact that he, like our cousin, was a natural bug boy while I was ... well ... not.

"Bugs crawl," I said, thinking that should explain everything about my aversion.

"They're supposed to crawl."

"Well, them crawling makes my skin crawl."

"Well, hardy har-har."

"Hey, hey, stop it, you two," my cousin said. "How come I'm the only one doin' the lookin' all of a sudden?" He'd been combing through the grass farther away from the tree trunk.

"I'm lookin', I'm lookin'," I said. But then I simply squatted down and brushed my hands over the thickening green blades, thinking only that soon it'd be time to cut all eight zillion of them again, and what a long, hot, boring time *that* would be.

Meanwhile, my brother tugged at a rock that was slightly buried in the ground. When he flipped it over, several gray pill bugs balled up protectively and a fat earthworm undulated, burrowing to escape the intrusion. I cringed at the sight of the worm,

Author at five years old.

remembering the last time I tried and failed to bait a hook with one when Dad took us fishing, which meant that Dad had to bait all my hooks for me. Of course, that didn't mean I didn't like fishing: I *loved* it, loved the excitement of feeling that tug on the line, loved reeling in my catch with one of the neat fishing poles Dad had made for us in his inimitably imaginative way, fashioning them out of narrow, smoothly sanded pieces of wood, some of Mom's empty sewing thread spools, and a few eye hooks. The reeled-in fish, usually a spot or croaker, would flop around in the boat, desperately clinging to life, its unblinking eyes always appearing to cry: *why, why, why?* But none of that ever bothered me. It was okay. Fish were okay. It was *worms* that weren't. Worms and bugs.

My brother picked up one of the pill bugs. He talked to it, toyed with it, let it crawl all over his hand like they were best buddies. It's a wonder he didn't lean down and give it a kiss.

So how come it wasn't just *him* hunting crickets for the turtle the way he usually did? Because he and my cousin thought it was time that I got over my fear of them. And besides, the turtle was as much mine as it was anyone else's. I was the one who'd found him, a rust-brown and dark-green box turtle snoozing peacefully under our back porch. And I really liked him. He was a pet, something you could pet, like a dog or rabbit or gerbil. Unlike bugs, who wouldn't stand for it, stay for it. Bugs weren't pets.

"Hey, guys, over here."

My brother dropped the pill bug and we went over to our cousin, who was at the grapevine that extended over part of the pathway leading from our back porch to the alley. He stood stock-still. Amid the sounds of a sputtering old car churning up gravel down the alley, some kids playing red light/green light several yards away, and birds sweetly chirping seemingly everywhere, one sound stood out in incredible relief: the unmistakable scissors-like screech-screeching of crickets.

"Okay, get ready." My cousin inched away a half-rotting plank leaning against one of the grapevine poles. The screeching stopped but there the crickets lay, three of them: big, black, ugly bugs.

I stared down at them, my heart pounding, my hands shaking once again. They seemed poised to attack. I imagined them as 50-foot mutants in some sci-fi horror movie. Actually, I really liked those kinds of movies because, curled up in the dark, munching popcorn and sipping soda in the com-

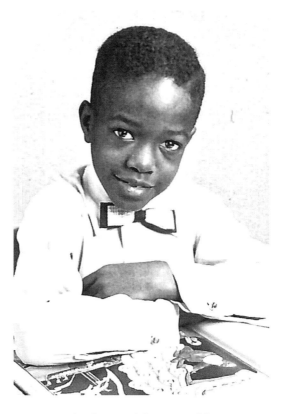

Author at eight years old.

fortable old Carver Theater, I could feel securely scared. And I could brazenly fantasize about being the brave hero saving the world from the terrible results of atomic experimentation; I could be James Arness, say, battling giant ants in *Them*, one of my all-time favorites, or Peter Graves—*Arness*'s younger brother, I later learned—taking on humongous grasshoppers in *Beginning of the End*. But at the moment, in the heat and humidity of ordinary life, all I could see myself as was the stupid little unheroic victim, the one who always dies an awful, gory death in the first ten minutes of all those movies.

"Go on," my cousin whispered.

"Quick, take your pick," prodded my brother.

"They won't hurt you."

"They're just dumb crickets."

"Go on."

I took a deep breath, and with my brow tightly knit and my eyes half-closed, I bent down and lunged at one of the creepy black things.

To my utter surprise I caught him, closing my right hand around him quickly. Meanwhile, the other two headed for cover. Wrong movie.

"All right!" my brother said.

My cousin patted me on the back. "You got him!"

"Yeah," I said, trying my best to feel triumphant. "I ... I got him."

I cupped my left hand under my right, creating as much space for the creature as I possibly could. He tickled my palms, his thin legs and antenna scratching to get free. I held on, but I was terrified. It was my first time. My very first time!

"Can't we get a jar or something?" I asked.

"Yeah, we'll get a jar," my cousin said. "Just bring him to the porch. And don't squeeze him to death."

"Yeah," my brother laughed. "The turtle won't eat no dead cricket, you know."

I imagined slimy cricket pus oozing out between my fingers. My stomach did a somersault.

My cousin headed for the back porch, my brother following him with an imitative swagger.

For *me*, however, walking wasn't so easy. After all, *I* had the cricket, who proceeded to churn his little legs more frantically with every step I took. He was clearly upset with being confined to shaky, sweaty human hands and wasn't going to go to his imminent death without a fight. I pictured him boring a hole in my palm, eating away at my flesh, and then swallowing me whole. To counter those horrid images I tried to think of the cricket's legs as grass, noodles, loose string, anything inanimate, "harmless."

It didn't work. Halfway to the back porch, I stopped.

"I can't, guys," I pleaded. "I just can't."

Simultaneously, two sets of shoulders slumped and turned back to me.

"Yes, you can," my cousin insisted. "Just keep your hands closed."

"No, I don't like this feeling. It doesn't feel right."

My brother rolled his eyes.

"I mean like... I... That is...." My mind raced, searching for a way out of my misery.

Author in snow with brother and sister.

"Let's just ... let's just feed the turtle lettuce. He can eat lettuce. He really likes lettuce. He loves it."

"Not as much as fat little crunchy crickets," my brother snickered.

That did it. I let the cricket go, shaking my hands as though I'd been stung by a bee. He escaped into the grass.

My cousin sighed, my brother sucked on his teeth. No one moved.

I swear I could hear crickets cackling.

Finally, I looked down at the ground. What else could I do? I felt really, really bad, especially in front of my cousin. He was fifteen, five years older than me, and I looked up to him. He was daring, confident, immensely athletic, and not just smart but also *street*-smart, all the things I felt that I wasn't—all the things that my younger brother was already cultivating. It didn't seem fair. Why was all that cool stuff blithely skipping over me as though I didn't exist?

Standing there before them, my body sweating from every single pore, I felt like this worthless, formless slab of gooey jelly.

Screech, screech, all right... Damn crickets.

II

Our backyard was teeming with crickets. In fact, it was a veritable nature preserve for all manner of tiny creatures, from buzzing beetles to speckled ladybugs to even the occasional praying mantis and garter snake. Wasps built their nests under the edges of our roof. Daddy longlegs bounded over tree branches and grass like tiny pebbles mysteriously brought to drunken life. Spiders of various shapes and sizes spun and caught and spun and caught. And at sunset, fireflies—we called them lightning bugs—coolly, benignly lit up the air, which made them the only bugs I gladly welcomed, happily observed, even collected, in glass jelly jars with tiny holes punched in their tops: our living, breathing lanterns.

It was a yard of rich soil as well, not only supporting the apple tree and the grapevine but also a cherry tree whose fruit we scrambled to pick in the spring before the birds got to them, a peach tree whose fruit never seemed to me to get ripe enough to ever be picked, an umbrella tree that was home to a leaf-eating mass of little cater-pillars every other year, and a maple tree I proudly transplanted from a local tree nursery on my twelfth birthday. There were also rows of hedges, a mulberry bush, and other greenery that at times seemed to sprout out of nowhere, like the tiny oak sapling that would keep growing and growing until one day—long after we'd moved away—it would dwarf everything in the yard, including the house.

And so there we were, my parents, my younger brother and sister and me—there in a middle-class Black neighborhood in the mid–1950s. There with all the crickets.

They even invaded my sleep: dreams of them crawling over me in bed, of them lifting me up from the top bunk and carrying me down the ladder and past my brother, who peacefully slept, oblivious to my cries for help. What did he care? Now he could have the whole room to himself while I'd be carried away to some giant cricket lair where I'd be slowly, painfully eaten alive for breakfast, lunch, and dinner.

Such dreams were bolstered by the knowledge that crickets even lived inside our house, in our damp basement, where they'd man-aged to squeeze through cracks in the stone walls and concrete floor or under the door that led outside. And at night if we went down there to retrieve some stored item—extra folding chairs, a mason jar of preserves, a hammer, a screwdriver, the ironing board—or to "light the tank," as soon as we opened the door the crickets would greet us with their high-pitched sounds. Whenever *I* had to go down there at night, I'd cringe for a moment at the top of the stairs and then creep down, the light turning on and the creak-creaking of my footsteps having stopped the crickets' screeching, but not necessarily having scared them away. It was as though I was expecting them to be waiting to see who was there, and when they saw it was me they'd simply wave their tiny antenna haughtily in the air as if to say: "Oh, never mind, it's just *him*." Hence, at the bottom stair, I'd also stomp my feet and shout to get them to know I meant business, you hear me, business!

But it was sort of okay in the basement during the day, when the crickets would stay away, hidden in the cool, dark nooks and crannies, sleeping perhaps, their little legs curled up under them, their little demon brains dreaming of more and more ingenious ways to taunt me. During the day my brother, sister, and I would have a great time down there fooling around, playing board games, searching through our parents' rapidly accumulating piles of "junk" for golden treasures, or just plain ole getting on each other's nerves.

More tellingly, though, was that during the day I would be bolder or more cavalier even on my own, like the time I was in the basement with a slightly younger friend, down there ostensibly to play. It was then that I coaxed him into doing the weird and forbidden, into pulling down his pants and his underwear, as I did the same. And we looked down at ourselves and our little penises, although since mine was erect, my friend felt moved to say, his eyes wide with wonder: "Boy, you sure got a big one." Me. Nine or ten years old and thinking of touching him and other boys, wanting to experiment with them, even though I was too scared to do much more than look for a few seconds and toy with touching. And besides, I was rather clumsy, inept at it all, a couple of times later being caught in the act of my heart-pounding looking, first by an aunt when I was in the shed with an older boy and then by my brother when I was in the bushes with one my own age. And both times my mother was told, my brother running so quickly to her that one would have thought I'd fallen down some deep, dark, dangerous well. Perhaps he'd simply been shocked or scared for some reason. We had never experimented like that, and we never would. In fact, the only relative I ever played doctor with was a female cousin around my age, and then only a couple of times.

I don't exactly remember what my mother said to me either

time, which had me much late substituting the stern look of disapproval I *do* remember getting from her with Paul Monette's mother's indelible "what were you doing with Kite" question that haunts him throughout most of his memoir, *Becoming a Man*. Both times I was terribly embarrassed and very contrite. And both times I promised her I'd never do "it" again.

I never heard from my father about what I'd done; perhaps my mother never told him. But when I was eighteen and had been away at college for about a month, I did get a letter from him warning me to beware of homosexuals in my dormitory. He was just looking out for me without having to look at me directly, I suppose, but his sweetly awkward letter—the only one more than a page long he ever wrote me, I think—unwittingly made me more frightened of *myself* than it did of any possible dormitory "predators."

III

Several years before my cricket safari fiasco, I fell in love with a boy for the first time. That is, I think I did, in retrospect. His name was Brian Hancock, which seems sort of funny, I suppose, but also only in retrospect. For as a sheltered seven year old, "cock" wasn't a word I knew, except during rampant games of cowboys and Indians. It was a time, you see, when every boy in the neighborhood, including cricket-averse me, had some sort of rifle or gun, and every single one of them was a toy that could be safely "cocked."

I would like to say that Brian had smooth, milk chocolate skin and sparkling brown eyes and an impish, dimply smile. I would like to say that we spent hours together in my room wrestling around on the floor, or hours sitting on the back porch projecting ourselves into the future, or hours in front of the TV mesmerized by cartoons and westerns, snuggling close together. I would *like* to say that. But

I can't. The truth is I don't remember much of anything about what Brian and I did together. And more strangely, I have no mental picture of him at all; I can't see him in my mind's eye the way I can see other friends from those early school years, especially girls, many of them pretty, with cute little curls and flirtatious smiles and nonchalant, matter-of-fact ways of touching me, getting close to me, next to me. I can see *them* easily, along with the wily faces of a couple of insouciantly gruff boys. But try as I might, I can't for the life of me see Brian.

Nonetheless, he was most definitely real, and I was deeply infatuated with him in a way that I wasn't with any other friend. I wouldn't have been able to name it as sexual then because I knew practically nothing about sex—didn't know what men and women did together in bed, didn't know where babies came from. I don't know if Brian or any of my other friends knew anything either, or my brother or sister. I never asked them. I didn't even ask my cousin or my parents. Maybe I didn't want to know, or was simply oblivious. It was like I was encased in my private little world of sensual feeling, and that was enough. Yet I suspect that a part of me at seven years old *did* know that the feelings I had for Brian went beyond just being pals, primarily because of the only two incidents involving him and me that I *do* remember.

The first one concerns a day when we were going to meet at lunchtime at school to play together. When that time came, however, I couldn't find him anywhere. Had he forgotten about me? Was he suddenly mad at me for some reason? More than halfway through the lunch hour I decided I'd go looking for him. An intrepid move for a seven year old. I walked up the avenue from the school toward his house. The walk turned out to be farther than I thought because I hardly ever walked that way from school, living as I did way in the opposite direction.

When I finally reached Brian's house, I discovered that he wasn't there. His mother told me that he was at school, which is where I should have been. By the time I got back to school I was fifteen minutes late and really embarrassed about having to walk into my second-grade class with everyone giving me those gleeful "awww, you're in trouble" sort of looks. I don't remember seeing Brian there; he may not have been in my class. But I do remember the teacher reprimanding me, being very disappointed in me, already one of the school's smartest, nicest, most well-behaved little boys. What could I have been thinking?

I don't know what explanation I gave her for my lateness. But what I'm certain of is that it was a lie, that I *didn't* say I'd been looking for Brian. Somehow I knew, or at least felt, that couldn't be an appropriate answer.

The second incident happened at my house. There was some kind of party. Several of my friends were over, and we'd been outside playing when suddenly I had to go to the bathroom to do what we euphemistically called "number two." While sitting upstairs on the toilet I heard Brian's voice in the hallway directly outside the bathroom door. I don't know why he was upstairs in my house: perhaps he'd been looking for me in my room. But the sound of his voice out there really excited me in a way I'd never felt before.

I called to him, asking him to come into the bathroom for a moment. When he opened the door I smiled at him, somewhat conspiratorially. He smiled back but didn't say anything. Neither did I at first. All I really wanted was for him to see me the way he'd never seen me before, with my pants and underwear down. Down legitimately, of course, since this was long before I had the temerity to do it any other way.

Finally, I said something stupid like: "Look what I'm doing." I don't think he had a reply. And he didn't come over to me or hang out or anything. Why would he have? He simply shrugged and left.

We never talked about it afterward, so I don't know what he felt about seeing me "naked." Maybe embarrassed. But I do know what *I* felt about his seeing me like that: all tingly inside.

Several months later Brian moved away with his family. I never saw or heard from him again, although strangely, rather eerily, much, much later, I did see his name on a list my mother had compiled of old friends to invite to my surprise eighteenth birthday party. I had no idea how she'd gotten his name, or even remembered him. But he didn't come. And now I sometimes achingly wonder what I would have done if he had.

IV

When I was twelve years old and headed for junior high school, I fell in love with a boy again—this time much more consciously. And although it wasn't love at first sight, when it fully registered, it was so palpable that it scared me to death.

His name was Michael Whitney, the fourteen-year-old older brother of a girl my age I had gone to elementary school with, and we were tent mates in Boy Scout camp.

In a way, my brother and I had been in the Boy Scouts even before we were old enough to join. Our dad was the Scoutmaster of the troop sponsored by our Baptist church, a troop he'd founded and was the driving force behind for years. All the boys loved my father, who was a kind, skillful, natural leader, and my brother and I were proud of the fact that he let us tag along on weekend overnight scouting trips in the country with those older boys, something other Cub Scouts never got to do. On those campouts we learned lots of things—how to pitch pup tents, dig trenches and latrines, build fires, tie various kinds of knots, identify trees and plants. Hence, later, when we became *real* Boy Scouts, we were ready for even bigger and better things: merit badge activities, jamborees, and the weeklong stays at official Boy Scout camps with other troops. What *I* wasn't ready for that summer, however, was Michael.

He was tall and skinny and darker than me, and he had an angular face, with long eyelashes that curled over dreamy brown eyes, the beginnings of a cute mustache, and lips that easily shaped themselves into a shy sort of smile. I was glad that we'd been assigned the same tent, even though he knew less about scouting than I did because he'd just joined the troop and had never gone camping. I liked him instantly, partly because despite those eyes he seemed tougher and more experienced than me, seemed almost ready for high school. In the five years since my first crush, I'd had enough experience with my body to know that my attraction to Michael had something to do with sex, with the things I used to innocently do with boys when I was still a mere Cub Scout but was now only doing with myself. But I immediately suppressed that sexual sense. Besides, there was too much to do that first day, too many things to adjust to at the camp; I could hardly see Michael for the woods. In addition, my dad was there—an advisor, friend, mentor to us all, and a second conscience, especially for me. That first night, however, exhausted and away from my father's watchful eye...

Well, the two-man tents at this camp were like palaces compared to the little pup tents our troop owned that we routinely pitched over plastic tarp laid out on the hard, cold ground. These tents were mounted on wooden platforms and were equipped with gray metal Army cots. It was like being in the lap of luxury. Michael, of course, didn't know this, so I had to explain it to him. I also joked about barely being able to see to get undressed in our sleeping bags between poles that helped prop up those little pup tents some of us could hardly sit up in, much less stand. In contrast, there we were, Michael and I, first standing, and then sitting down on our respective beds, with a bright lantern shining overhead. Admittedly the cots were only about two feet apart, but they were also at least two feet above natural bug level, which was fine with me, although I didn't speak a word about that part to Michael.

Michael's eyes had brightened a little at my tiny tale of "roughing it." Finally, he smiled his great smile. I smiled back. Then, my center involuntarily tingling, I sheepishly looked away toward the closed front flaps of our tent. When I looked back, Michael simply sighed and sort of half-shrugged, although I had no idea why. Then he did something that, despite the fact that it was close to lights-out time, I hadn't for the life of me anticipated. He got up and nonchalantly proceeded to undress—right in front of me. My body flinched, then froze up. Soon he was absolutely naked. And that's when my attraction kicked in so completely that my heart nearly lodged in my throat. All I could do was stare at his beautiful body, and more specifically at his penis, which seemed much bigger than mine and had more hair around it.

Now I'd seen naked boys before, but only briefly while quickly changing in locker rooms at the public swimming pool or at the beach. (I had yet to tackle showers after gym class in junior high school.) And I'd seen my brother and my father naked a few times. But here was a boy I was already viscerally drawn to on some level standing in all his glory so casually close to me that I could reach out and touch him, which right then I so longed to do. I was suddenly in love.

He shivered a little and hugged himself, commenting about how cool it had gotten. I limply agreed, wondering if he could see the blush that had heated my face. Then he casually turned away from me and searched for his pajamas. When he found them and began putting them on, I came to my senses. I turned away from him and fumbled for my own pajamas, then struggled out of my clothes and into those pajamas *over* my underwear, hoping Michael didn't think me uncool to do so while at the time same fighting like hell to hide the erection I'd gotten. Then it was lights out and goodnight, us lying on the springy mattresses of our parallel cots, lying under dull-green wool Army blankets to protect us from that cool night air, even though the last thing I was feeling was cool. Michael seemed to fall asleep easily enough, but I lay awake for a long time that night, my head spinning, my heart occasionally skipping beats—lay awake wrestling with the sudden, astronomical progression of my attraction and how I might somehow wish it away, or at least control it, keep it from spilling over into some action I was certain would be my ruin.

Well, control it I did, first by being sure never to completely undress in front of Michael or be caught again watching him do so in front of me, which took some odd maneuvering at times. I also kept myself busy, which wasn't very hard to do at a camp defined by constant activity. Michael and I did do things together, but we did many more things with others in the troop, and I always made sure that I kept my hands to myself, so to speak.

There was one time, however, when the depths of my longing came crashing down heavily upon me. I was in my tent with the flaps closed because I was changing into my swimming trunks for the day's afternoon swim when suddenly I heard a group of boys laughing and fooling around in the adjacent tent. Soon I realized that they were cavalierly talking about their dicks and about when and how they got hard—looking at pictures or seeing girls on the street or simply waking up in the morning. I pressed an ear to the canvas tent wall, straining to hear more, to take in every detail. There were boys in that tent I hadn't thought much about beyond our casual friendship and the scouting stuff we participated in … but was Michael there?

Soon that tent grew quiet. All I could hear was the pounding of my heart amid the typical forest sounds shot through with some distant camp activity. Then a few muffled but very distinct "oh, wows" and "yeahs" seeped through to me. My pulse raced even more, and I *put* Michael there, *saw* him there, displaying his erection along with others. And I wanted so much to join him, join all of them, wanted to share with everyone my own arousal. The strength in numbers would have made it okay to expose myself to the boy I'd fallen in love with.

But I didn't, of course. Didn't race over there shouting, "me, too, me, too!" That would have been too stupid, obvious, insistent. Instead, I resigned myself later to watching some of them exit that tent sporting lingering little swimming-trunk tents of their own. It seemed to be no big deal to them—no big deal, in fact, to anyone but me. Meanwhile, Michael bopped down a path from the woods, already dressed for swimming, a shy, what-did-I-miss sort of smile creasing his handsome face.

During the remainder of my stay at Boy Scout camp—when not eating or swimming or hiking or competing, including winning the knot-tying contest—I soothed my sexual desires by settling for a couple of furtive, solitary rounds of masturbation in the enclosed little wooden latrine, engulfed by images of Michael, burning with overwhelming feelings I all the while berated myself for having.

Ironically, after Boy Scout camp I never saw Michael again. He abruptly dropped out of the scouts for some reason. I asked his sister about him a couple of times when I ran into her, but I never called him, nor did he call me. Besides, we lived in different neighborhoods, went to different schools, and he was quickly too old for me anyway. But somewhere in my head—much, much more than with Brian—Michael became a kind of symbol of missed opportunity, a representation of a longing that somehow indelibly imprinted itself on the back of my heart, an imprint that seemed, in retrospect, to capture and corral a part of me and keep it permanently fixed at that ripe young age of twelve.

V

Four years later I strikingly fell in love with a boy yet again. This time it was a love even more solidly, perhaps sickeningly unrequited, for the boy was in a black and white photograph on a page of a yearbook volume of my family's *World Book Encyclopedia*. He was a white boy, barefoot, blond, and dressed in a striped T-shirt and white shorts. The photo, which graced the first page of a long section on children and health, had captured that boy, who seemed to be about my age, mid-stride as he happily jumped over a white girl, also happy and blond and in her teens. She wore a white jumpsuit and crouched down to the ground as though she and her friend were playing a game of leapfrog. There was nothing sexual about the boy and girl's connection or about the text that surrounded the picture: it was a pitch for healthy exercising among young people. But because the boy's legs and arms were spread the way a hurdler's would be, I could see in the shadow made by his open pant leg at his crotch ... whatever my imagination called me to see.

I fixated on that photograph for most of my junior year in high school, sneaking looks at it alone in my room, as though it were a *Playboy* centerfold or some blatant piece of pornography. Not that I'd ever seen a *Playboy* centerfold, much less pornographic pictures. The only time, in fact, that I'd longingly eyed a pulsating picture of a man and woman was when my brother and I, when we were thirteen and fifteen respectively, went to see a movie downtown whose name I can't recall. The previews before that movie I vividly remember, however. They were for a new film called *Splendor in the Grass*, starring Natalie Wood and newcomer Warren Beatty, and included a brief shot of the two of them hotly grappling, and seemingly naked to me, under a waterfall. I was both surprised and turned on, and I'm sure my brother was, too. But we said nothing to each other; we didn't even look at each other. We simply sat through our movie and then silently waited for its next scheduled showing just to see the previews once again, after which we got up and left the theater, again without saying anything. Near nakedness in the dark twice in one sitting, exciting but forbidden in our world, with me eyeing Beatty as much as I eyed Wood, doubly forbidden. Of course, the boy in the encyclopedia also wasn't naked. Besides, it wasn't about nakedness for me: it was about *him*.

Sometimes I even masturbated in the bathroom to that picture, fantasizing about this boy I didn't know, fantasizing because I knew that it was safe to do so, that I couldn't have him, touch him, be with him in any way. He was a clear substitute for the real thing, for in high school there was no particular boy to whom I even allowed myself to be more than fleetingly attracted, much less to pine for. And although I dated a girl or two, there wasn't much pining there, either.

There *was* another photograph in that health section that I felt oddly drawn to, by the way—one that seemed to have been taken from a medical journal. It was an old print of a sickly looking boy being comforted by a physician. The boy was about eleven or twelve and was suffering from smallpox or some other dreaded disease. And he was naked, except that the picture was cropped just above his genitals. I rarely turned the page to look at that boy, however, because I was much more ambivalent and

Author in high school graduation photograph.

confused about my attraction to him. His being younger and in need of comfort slightly repulsed me. Yet when I focused more closely on his eyes, I sensed that that youth and need were the things about him that also aroused me. The boy, in fact, looked too much like what I sometimes felt like inside.

But my "happy hurdler" was my current ideal—my white Michael, perhaps. I'd fallen in love with a pose, a potential, something arrested—arrested both on that glossy page of a so-called book of knowledge and yet again as an incredible kind of longing in my heart.

VI

During my freshman year in college that longing caused me to steer clear of morning showers in my dormitory because to my horror there were no individual shower stalls, with or without plastic curtains, and I was deathly afraid of being aroused around and/or by other guys. (The bathroom stalls were also merely tiled cubicles open in the front, which meant having to do "number two" in rather plain view, although in my paranoia that design seemed specifically aimed at me and my masturbatory habits, which had become rampant.) Of course, there'd been open showers in my high school, but there, in everyone's rush to get to the next class after gym, I had learned to cope reasonably well. The dormitory, however, was my new home: I *lived* there with all these guys, these boys to men.

Such fear kept me from taking showers daily. And when I did take one, I would wait until the late afternoon, or some other irregular time. Only my roommate seemed to take note once or twice of my odd showering habits. But since he was an arrogant, sneering white boy who'd complained behind my back to his parents the first day of school about having the misfortune of having to room with "him," one of only eleven Black students out of 2000 in the freshman class, I

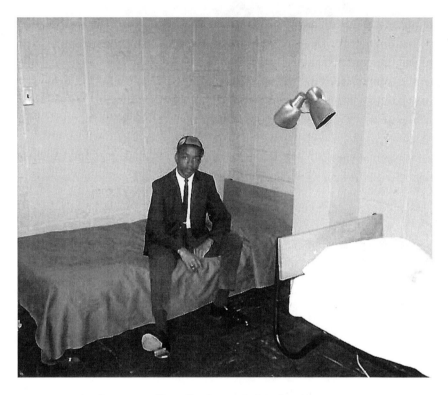

Author as a college freshman in his dormitory room.

didn't like him very much, was in no way attracted to him, and didn't much care what he thought about me.

In any event, to take a shower, I'd "sneak" into the bathroom, my underwear and shorts still on, my towel and toiletries in my arms, and hope to God that I didn't hear water running just around the corner from the urinals, cubicles, and mirrors. If I did hear it, at times accompanied by some guy blithely singing or a couple of guys casually conversing, I would hang back, pretending to have business in front of the mirror, or sadly slink back to my room and wait. And if the coast was clear, I would hurry into the shower, scrubbing and cleaning with alacrity, so glad to be finally naked under cascades of soothing water, which gave me such sensual pleasure that I had to work even harder not to think of boys and the control my penis seemed to constantly have over me.

I was a horny eighteen year old who was angry, alone, and terribly frustrated and confused, for I had thought that going away to college, powered by high school achievements and multiple scholarships and happy to be away from DC and my family, would make me feel freer to express myself, find out more about who I was, not keep me trapped in my own skin. Yes, I liked boys, but I felt I had nowhere to go with that reality beyond my fantasies, and I fought like hell to keep the label "homosexual" out of my consciousness, even when it appeared vividly on the page, as it did in my dad's letter. Besides, I liked girls, too—in some ways more than I did boys. Yet I also feared them as much as I feared boys, feared failing them. And even though I was soon to have a real girlfriend in DC, a smart, independent Black girl who'd gone to junior high with my brother and had been a year behind me in my high school, our relationship, because she'd go on to a different college from me, was rather distant, often more ambivalent than intimate. Meanwhile, at my college, I was wary of all intimacy, keeping to myself emotionally and developing few friendships beyond some of the guys I met on my dormitory floor or in Air Force ROTC.

In an odd way, ROTC was a kind of haven for me, despite the antiwar movement's beginning to heat up on college campuses. It was a place where I could hang out and be just one of the guys. Yet it wasn't a fraternity. Not that I didn't consider joining one of them. I checked out a couple in the spring and was accepted as a pledge by one. But finally I declined their offer because I once again feared the kind of casual intimacy that would be a part of living so closely with a group of guys. But guys didn't live together in ROTC, they simply did things together. Besides, as a male, I could substitute it at the university for the two required years of physical education. And of course,

ROTC was at least something that I knew—having been a top junior ROTC cadet in high school. There was something, I suppose, actually comforting about the discipline, defined roles, and precision that were important parts of this training ground for future military officers. That first year I even joined—and excelled in—the ultra-precise and disciplined drill team. I was one of the guys, you see, one of the boys in Air Force ROTC... And so, appropriately enough, my next "boy crisis" came in that arena.

In the spring of my sophomore year I was offered a full-tuition Air Force ROTC scholarship if I'd enroll in the advanced program my junior and senior year, a program that would lead to my being commissioned an officer upon graduation and being committed to at least four years of military service. I already had a medley of college scholarships that paid most of my tuition, but one full-tuition award would be simpler and more complete, and I liked the idea of going into the military as an officer in the Air Force—although not as a pilot since I was too nearsighted—rather than sweating over possibly being drafted into the Army after graduation. But a couple of days before I was to sign a letter of commitment, I panicked. Suddenly, all I could see, all I could feel about me, was my same-sex attraction. How could I be a decent, moral leader of men if I was continually lusting after boys? For the first time I saw beyond the casual camaraderie of ROTC activities to that which had kept me from pledging a fraternity or taking daily showers my first year in college—despite the fact that I was now relaxed about the latter as a result of living in dorms whose bathrooms had individual, curtained shower stalls. I pictured basic training, close quarters, and more open showers, where I would stumble upon another Michael and be thoroughly humiliated, branded a pervert. Hence, with my shame and paranoia working overtime and feeling that I was undeserving of a ROTC scholarship, I went to the commandant of cadets and respectfully declined the Air Force's offer, citing "personal matters," without further explanation. The commandant was utterly dismayed. But I told myself that for the first time in my life I was taking into account the possibility that I was gay, even though I didn't want to be, even though I felt more afraid than honorable.

Late that night, very depressed and filled with self-hatred, I impulsively slammed out of my dormitory and walked down the hill from the university into the city proper, walked without knowing precisely where I was going, walked as though all I wanted to do was walk away from myself, walk out of my life, just walked and walked until I came by chance upon a local bar, at which point I did something I'd never done before: I walked right in on my own.

I must have been a curious sight—this barely twenty-year-old Black kid, who looked all of perhaps seventeen, strolling into a smoke-filled bar of old regulars close to midnight in the middle of the week, sitting down on a barstool as though he had all the experience in the world, and then half-stumbling over his ordering of a beer. Since the drinking age in New York State was still eighteen and I had my student ID and my driver's license on me, the bartender had to serve me. Meanwhile, everyone else had returned to their conversations or their watching of some late-night movie on the overhead TV. And that was fine with me. I had no interest in talking to anyone: I could barely make eye contact. I simply wanted to drown myself in drink—whatever that meant. But since I wasn't much of a drinker, I could only make it through about two bottles of beer before I began to feel dizzy and high. And since I also didn't want to add insult to injury by getting sick in the bar, I went to the bathroom, peed, and splashed water on my face. Then I stared at myself in the mirror over the sink, a mirror that was so scratched and dirty it only served to reinforce my quandary... Who or what the hell was I and where was I headed?

I left a generous tip at the bar, which rendered me practically broke, and walked out into the cool night air, its sting helping to prop me up. Off in the distance up the hill the lights of the university shined like unwanted beacons, but I had to go back. My sexual confusion and loneliness had made me miserable in college off and on over the past two years, but I had to go back, had to walk back, had to finish, to take it like a man, even if I was far from feeling like one.

As I walked down the dimly lit street, a lone car that had just passed by me going in the opposite direction suddenly slowed down, made a U-turn, and pulled up to the curb beside me. Rather than keep walking I stopped, more bewildered than alarmed. What had I done now?

The driver rolled down his curbside window. I bent over a bit and peered in at a clean-shaven white man, dressed casually, who seemed to be in his early forties. He asked me if I needed a ride. With half a shrug and not much thought I said, "yeah." And then I did another thing I'd never done before: I got in a stranger's car.

He asked me where I was going, I told him to the university, and he headed down the street.

For an awkward moment neither of us spoke. I was tired and my head was buzzing, and he seemed content with concentrating just on driving. Yet I had this weird feeling that he was also staring at me.

Finally, after what sounded like a quick intake of air on his part, this average-looking white man driving this average-looking car asked me, almost in a whisper, if I'd ever given anybody a blow job.

His question jolted me, sent a shiver down my spine. But more important than that was what it didn't do. It didn't cause me to scream at him: "Stop this damn car and let me the hell out, you fucking pervert!" For it seemed to me that this man had somehow homed in on me, homed in on who I was or was rapidly becoming, and had every right to ask me that question. And almost instantly I got an erection, which to me was further proof of the man's right, proof of his insight.

The car seemed to move more slowly now, seemed to be silently floating on air, saturated with the smell of desire and hermetically sealed against intrusion, or rescue, from the outside world. My throat was dry, my heart pounding, my skin prickly.

Finally, I answered his question in the only way I could—with a near breathless "no."

Another charged moment of silence ensued. I refused to look at the man, but I was certain now that he was staring at me—staring at a Black boy he lusted after as much as I at times lusted after boys. Then just as my throbbing penis jerked against the waistband of my underpants, he asked me if I got lots of hard-ons.

Inside, I laughed, but the irony was too frightening to sustain that laughter for more than a millisecond. Outwardly, all I could do was slowly swallow and nod, saying, very softly, "yes." Quickly, as though roused by anticipation, he asked me if I had a hard-on right then. Mechanically, I nodded again and said "yes." And he said quite sharply: "Let me see."

With that he reached over with his right hand, his left hand still steering the car down the dark, empty street, and unzipped my pants, pulled my penis out of my underwear, and began stroking it.

Suddenly, I was dizzy again, but I didn't say "stop" or push his hand away because this time I was dizzy with pleasure and longing. I wanted him to go on, to go even farther. I wanted him to take me with him to wherever he wanted to go. His lonely bachelor's pad or some bleak motel room or even some dark alley. Anyplace where I could easily touch him as well. In fact, I wanted to reach over and touch him right then, to stroke his penis, which I imagined was also erect. I wanted to kiss him, wanted to give him a blow job, wanted to have sex with him, to have my first sex ever. And I wanted him to hold me, squeeze me, love me, for although he wasn't someone like Michael, although he clearly wasn't a boy, I was twelve years old again and wanted to be *his.*

In that moment of reverie, I was completely at that stranger's mercy. He could easily have driven me into the woods and then raped and killed me. I could have disappeared without a trace, which in large part was the reason I'd walked down the hill from the university in the first place.

But it was only a moment, for soon he abruptly stopped stroking me and put my still-erect penis back into my underwear without saying a word. No apology, no "let's wait until we get to my place," no "you disgust me, all of a sudden." He simply kept driving, this time clearly driving me up the hill toward the university.

I sat immobile again for a second or two, still partially exposed, then fumbled with my pants to zip up. And rather than feel grateful I felt rejected, felt that I had failed him, had failed to respond, even though I'd so much wanted to. I was a coward. I was someone who'd turned down a full scholarship because of what he felt inside and yet when the opportunity arose to act on those feelings, sat frozen with further fear.

As he drove, the man seemed to relax out of his own fear. Maybe it had been his first time as well—his first time picking up a boy on the street, his first time touching a boy's body like that. Maybe he was actually married with kids of his own back home. Yet he seemed not to be able to shake his feelings so easily, any more than I could mine, for he began probing again, searching at least for titillation, this time asking about the sexual habits of the guys in my dorm. Did they jerk off a lot? Did they ever jerk off together? Did they...? Did they...?

Unwilling to allow myself to be aroused again, my flat answer to all of his questions was that I didn't know, I didn't really know.

When he pulled up to the front of my dorm, I peered at him for the first time since I'd gotten into his car. He seemed as sad and

Author as a college senior in his dormitory room.

lonely as I felt. I half-smiled and thanked him for the ride. He said "sure," without smiling. Then I got out and closed the door. And he drove off.

Needless to say, I never saw him again.

As soon as I got into my pajamas and settled into bed in my dorm room I broke down. I tried to cover my sobs to keep from possibly embarrassing myself, but my despair was too much to bear. Soon my big, sleek Polish roommate, a bright political science major who'd washed out of football as a wide receiver the year before, woke up and gently asked me if I was okay. And although we weren't really close because he was a junior and I a sophomore and we only shared the same space by random assignment because neither of us had managed to put in a request for a certain roommate the year before, I was too tired and whipped not to answer him with a frank, simple "no." He asked me if I wanted to talk, and again I simply said, "no." And then after a moment, in a tone of real concern, he suggested that I go see the dean of the university's chapel. Who knows what my roommate was thinking, what he was surmising about me, but at that point I didn't care. I just thanked him and, emotionally spent, rolled off to sleep.

The very next afternoon, having gotten an appointment at the last minute and feeling emboldened and ready to open up, I walked into the hearty, much-beloved dean's plush office and sat down. He was quite warm and welcoming. But after introductions and pleasantries, my plans for true confession flew completely out the window. Oh, I did tell him about my decision not to enter advanced ROTC and how it had to do with certain sexual concerns. But instead of moving into talking about my attraction to guys, I talked about my preoccupation with sex in general and about concerns about excessive masturbation. I even spun into fantasy, telling him that I was worried that I might have contracted VD—even though, unbeknownst to him, I was still a virgin. In fact, I did everything I could to help him label me as "normal," which he promptly did with wit and sensitivity, advising me to simply get tested for VD if I felt I should and then stop worrying about what I did with myself. After all, I was young, vibrant. He said that he was certain I would make a fine Air Force officer, if that's what I really wanted to be. I nodded and nodded and even laughed a little. Then, as I was preparing to leave, he asked me if that was all, if there wasn't anything else that was bothering me, that was on my mind. I just looked at him for a moment, this easygoing man of the cloth, someone who seemed to be genuinely on my side. It was almost … almost as though he knew, or at least had an inkling, but was leaving it to me to broach the subject. And once again, I failed: I was too afraid to completely open up, even to him. I told him, no, that was it. Then I got up, shook his hand, thanked him, and left.

The next morning, with some apology about any problems I'd caused, I signed the letter of intent that would give me my full-tuition scholarship and lead me to being commissioned as a second lieutenant in the Air Force. I was okay, you see. Not because I'd decided through some epiphany that it was all right to be gay, to like boys. I was okay because I really wasn't all that gay. After all, I liked girls, too, regardless of how virginal I still was. And I didn't really like boys all that much, *because* of how virginal I still was.

Author in college graduation photograph.

Yes, I was okay, I was okay. I was lying to myself, for inside I was still principally lonely, depressed, obsessed. But outside I was fucking A-OK.

VII

I finally did lose my virginity, at twenty-three, to my girlfriend from DC, although we broke off our short-lived engagement a few months afterward. I was still too closed off for her, I think. And too ambivalent.

Through graduate school and the Air Force and further graduate school, through living in Texas and Chicago and New York, I slept with more women and eventually a few men as well, acknowledging a kind of bisexuality in my soul. But through all that sexual discovery one particular desire, the longing for boys, inexplicably anchored itself even more strongly in my psyche, sometimes going dormant, other times flaring up like some sort of chronic disease, seeming to have no remedy in my intimacies with either men or women. Eventually, the mere sight of the *word* "boy" could arouse me, tear at my soul like any image in full view or tapped via my memory of Brian or Michael or whomever.

In my late twenties the pressure, the fear of acting out, became so great that I finally sought advice, help, therapy. I talked and talked and read and read, searching for answers, for ways to cope, strategies to keep myself from falling into the awful abyss, from becoming dismally criminal.

Meanwhile, my fundamental life continued to be exemplary, to remain very safe, sound, solid. I even fell truly in love and got married, had two beautiful daughters. But after nearly twenty years of what was principally a wonderful, caring partnership, I finally forced myself to come to terms with my sexuality, which allowed me to fully come out, which led to a difficult but ultimately amicable divorce. And now...

VIII

Sometimes I wonder whether I'd have boldly braved the basement at night, ignoring the crickets and their screeching, if I could have gone down there with Brian or Michael or some other boy, wonder whether I would have gladly held a cricket in one hand, ignoring its scratchy entreaties, if I could have held and gently squeezed a boy's hand in my other, wonder what it really means, in fact, to be a brave little boy. Wherein does such bravery lie? And how does one touch it, hold it in one's hand?

Perhaps if I'd had a cricket of another sort when I was a boy. A cuddly, kind sort of Jiminy Cricket. He would have come to me and whispered in my ear as I grew into adolescence, assuring me that *all* love could be good, that it was okay to be who I was, feel what I felt, dream what I dreamed. Or am I simply wishing to have changed something that was indeed there all along: a punishing, superego-tripping sort of Jiminy Cricket, constantly shaking one of his scratchy fingers at me or sniffing at me with his probing antenna, threatening to swallow me whole if I didn't stop, screech-screeching in my ear over and over and over again: "Beware, beware...."

IX

I never did manage to catch a cricket for our turtle. Ever. But he didn't seem to mind: my brother was always so accommodating. And my brother eventually stopped getting on my case about being afraid to pick up bugs. After all, there were things that he was afraid of back then, too, like not growing out of his habit of wetting the bed. Even my self-assured, worldly cousin had his fears, I'm sure. Hell, we all have fears. Some we grow out of, others we don't. Just as with feelings.

I can now pick up a bug or two without freaking out. But I still can't hold a cricket in my hand, will never be able to, I don't think. It just doesn't feel right. I no longer fear them, however: I simply acknowledge their right to exist in the world, honor their place in nature. At the same time, I know that I'll never eradicate my attraction to boys, whomever else I should fall in love with. And I'm trying to no longer fear that as well—or hate myself for it. I live with it without action, accept it as something that exists, that's a part of me, for whatever reason, controlled, arrested, in a good way. Or call it incongruously frozen, if you will—frozen to be endlessly studied and written about perhaps, like the complex, imagined feelings emanating from those lovers in John Keats's "Ode on a Grecian Urn."

Ironing

Ironing has always been as much a ritual as a necessity for me. Which is why I carried it with me when I went away to college. A ritual from home. One that, although my desire-for-independence self didn't realize it then, helped to anchor and comfort me, to wrest some sense of order out of the chaos of my new life, even as I risked ridicule by engaging in it, the ironing board being in the common laundry room in the basement of my freshman dorm.

Most of the guys in my dorm, as far as I could tell, never ironed anything. The rich preppy kids sent their shirts to the cleaners, the would-be hippies didn't give a damn, and those who were neither or both ... well, I don't know. But there I was, nonetheless, after having washed and dried a load of clothes, setting aside my shirts and pants—jeans were not yet ubiquitous—opening up the ironing board, and ironing my clothes with the simple little travel iron my maternal grandmother had given me.

First, in preparation, I'd lightly sprinkle each shirt with water and wrap it into a tight ball. Then I'd iron each one beginning with the sleeves. Then I'd do the collar, then the top part of the shirt placed around the narrow end of the board—one, two, three, four moves of the shirt between presses of the iron. And finally, the body of the shirt, button-hole portion first, then the back in two or three moves, and lastly the part with the buttons, maneuvering smartly around each one. With the pants I'd start with the waist positioned around the board's narrow end, making sure that the pockets lay flat underneath. Then the pant legs along the length of the board, inseam side of each first, being careful with the creases, then the pants pressed together on each side, again keeping the creases straight, pressing extra hard on the cuffs, if there were any. Sometimes I'd even iron my T-shirts, although I drew the line at my undershirts and shorts, despite the fact that I'd seen my father iron his own from time to time.

It felt so soothing, this ironing, so soothing seeing the wrinkles disappear. Ritual and comfort. The tactile sense of things smoothing out, working out, taking proper shape. It was a sense not unlike the one I'd get whenever my dad cut my hair, haircuts which were destined to be more and more infrequent with my being away at college and moving farther away from home, the intervals between returns turning into months at times, until finally haircuts from my dad stopped altogether, my having found some reliable other barber, or a series of them, although in no way surrogate dads.

My father's cutting my hair was the most tactile connection I had with him when I was growing up. The sitting on the stepstool on old newspaper spread out on the dining room floor, the wrapping and safety-pinning of the sheet around me, with me involuntarily flinching every time even though I knew Dad's finger always protected me from possibly getting stuck by that pin. Then the buzz of the little motor, the movement of the shears along my scalp, the careful clip-clip of the scissors, my dad's gentle maneuvering of my head, his casual breath on the nape of my neck. The closeness and quietude of it all. Quiet because we rarely spoke of things during this time, rarely revealed much more of each other to each other beyond our silent, assumptive love for each other. Unlike what went on in our lively neighborhood barbershop on Nichols Avenue, also a place of ritual, but a place from which my brother and I stopped receiving haircuts when as a four- or five-year-old I got a mild case of impetigo,

a contagious but easily treatable skin disease, possibly from said barbershop, and my dad, true to his talent and ingenuity—along with
the memory of what his own dad used to do—bought himself hair
clippers and other barber equipment and taught himself how to cut
hair, eventually cutting not only mine and my brother's but other
interested male relatives as well. Haircutting as a service and a gift.
Just like my dad. And also, of course, a kind of shaping up. Just like
ironing.

The reason I could iron with such unapologetic ease at eighteen
was that my brother, sister, and I grew up ironing our own clothes.
That was simply one of the chores we were responsible for in our
household as soon as we were old enough to learn how. No distinc-
tions made between the girl and the two boys. After all, our father
ironed his clothes. He also cooked and washed dishes, just like our
mother. Of course, we weren't required to cook, but we were required
to clean the kitchen after meals, which was at times the cause of
much contention among us three. We tried several ways of dividing
up that chore. We created three activities: washing the dishes, dry-
ing and putting them away, and taking out the garbage and the trash,
each of us taking one job, with the grudging concession that that
third job, although "yucky," took up the least amount of precious kid
time. Then we tried rotating among the jobs daily. Then we tried each
week. Then contemplated but I think rejected each month. Then we
tried one person doing all three jobs one day and having two days off.
We kept charts and schedules. But still we argued. Someone missed
a day; someone didn't finish a job; someone was too slow, which held
up the other two; someone pleaded with someone to stand in for
him or her because of heavy homework or a favorite TV show, which
caused cross-outs and confusion in the posted schedule. We'd even
taunt whoever had the dreaded dishwashing duty with silly singsong
chants and finger pointing. But through all the bickering and some
admonitions from our parents, we generally kept the kitchen neat

and clean, and unwittingly, even if just implicitly, absorbed how good it felt in the end to do so. And that's probably why I tend to obsess over keeping my kitchen clean to this day, why I readily took on the responsibility of washing the dishes and cleaning the kitchen in my marriage, why I sometimes even feel the urge to clean others' dirty kitchens as well when I encounter them. The act of cleaning, of washing, wiping, and putting things in their proper place can be as much of a soothing ritual to me as ironing.

But ironing in its strictest sense aside, I've always had the impulse and desire to smooth out wrinkles, or their equivalent in my eyes: pages carelessly folded back in magazines, books misaligned on bookshelves, pictures slightly off kilter, shoelaces untied. Things often have to be "just so"—in my connotative meaning of that phrase. Although not nearly as hard-core as with my paternal grandmother, who kept an immaculate home where absolutely everything had its proper place, including dessert, which had to be served *directly* after dinner, regardless of whether or not one was ready to eat it then. And it's not that I'm incapable of leaving messes or that I suffer from obsessive-compulsive disorder or have some kind of fabulous fashion sense. It's more that I'd rather not *see* things messy, which of course can lead to wanting things—myself included—to be seen as perfect, which at times has caused more problems than it's solved.

For example, when I was in elementary and junior high school, where good penmanship—which sounds like a military term to me now—was stressed by some of my teachers, I was criticized more than once for having too many cross-outs on my papers: they made them too messy. But what those teachers failed to understand was that I *had* to cross out certain words because they already looked messy to me, because they weren't yet perfectly written. And that need for my idea of visual perfection insured that the mechanical drawing class I took in high school would both soothe me and obsess me.

Mechanical drawing was an elective course that was meant, like home economics and typing, to give one practical skills in preparation for some career. And our teacher, a bespectacled, balding, rounded-shouldered white man with slightly beady eyes and a rather drone-like voice, was necessarily a stickler for straight lines, proper scaling, and perfect lettering. The assignments required meticulous care and a steady hand, along with a sense of perspective and design, or at least order, which created the challenge for me of relying on my drive for perfection, for perfect alignments, if you will, without allowing that drive to send me over the cliff into the valley of dread, where no drawing was ever finished, ever good enough to hand in. Yet when I was in the middle of an assignment and at one with my rulers and angles and compasses, with my mechanical pencil and my steady hand, I was in heaven, in a state of ecstasy that took me away from all the high school messiness through which I had to wade. Hence, it mattered less to me in mechanical drawing than in any other class I took that I didn't always get an A on my assignments, for I would already have had the cliché of a kind of Zen experience in the process of completing them. Calming, soothing, near perfect.

A much earlier activity that produced, indeed required, such Zen-like qualities as a part of its structure was a business venture my brother and I were involved in one summer with our older cousin Gerald. Pooling our money, we'd sent away for a kit of flexible rubber molds of popular cartoon characters such as Mickey Mouse, Goofy, Elmer Fudd, and Donald Duck, each about three inches high. Our goal was to make plaster figurines, paint them, and go throughout the neighborhood selling them as knick-knacks from a homemade cardboard display case that hung with string around one of our necks. Our asking price was 15 cents each, two for 25. Unfortunately, we didn't make as much of a profit as we'd hoped, although many folks were so pleased with our enterprising nature that they bought a knick-knack or two even though it was tacitly clear to us they had no intension of ever displaying them, at least not prominently.

But the real challenge wasn't in the selling anyway: it was in the making. Each plaster figurine had to be meticulously painted, although buyers turned a blind eye to one or two running colors or slightly off-center facial features. But even before a figurine could be deemed worthy of painting it had to "emerge" from its mold in perfect condition, which meant that the plaster of Paris had to be mixed perfectly, not too lumpy or thick yet not so thin that it wouldn't properly set in the mold. It also had to be poured into the mold with dispatch, before it began to set up in the mixing bowl. And then would come the Zen part—although not even our teenage cousin called it that. Peeling the rubber mold off a cartoon guy without damaging him required great care and patience. And that required, as one of us, usually Gerald, slowly peeled off a mold, that we all chant a kind of "song of perfection" we'd invented strictly for the occasion, our little hearts pounding in anticipation. It was both scary and quite tantalizing, and when we failed, oh so frustrating. A nicked ear here, a damaged foot there. But we kept at it, until another school year began, anyway. And, as a result, that summer I think I learned more about ritual and care and meticulous work than I had in all my previous ones.

Even more, perhaps, than I did when we made paint-by-number pictures, an activity that was all the craze in middle-class America in the 1950s. Kits with two little paint brushes and lots of premixed, numbered paints ready to be applied to numbered spaces on an accompanying canvas. Right up my creative little alley it was, then. Or perhaps my little creative alley. Order, precision, patience. Neat and clean and correct. Simply follow directions, stay meticulously within the lines, and as a reward for being so "good," *voilà*: a beautiful picture, whole and almost exclusively "naturalistic."

I didn't obsess all that much over paint by numbers, however;

after a couple of them I lost interest. At bottom, they required too much of my kid time. And, of course, it was only decades later that I learned that I had been a tiny part of a "mindless conformity" movement, one that supposedly helped coin the expression, often used pejoratively, "doing things by the numbers."

But my meticulousness found other ways to manifest itself. For example, when I learned in the Boy Scouts the military-corner way to make a bed, I right away claimed it as my own and took great pains to make my bed that way every time, even at home. I was also very good in the Scouts at tying very quickly and efficiently all manner of special knots. And when I was a nineteen-year-old bus boy one summer in a federal government cafeteria—my second summer working in such a cafeteria—regular bus boys would marvel at how neat the shelves of my metal bus truck were. That is, how did I manage to find the time, amid the hustle-bustle pressure of having to clear and clean tables at lunchtime while hungry employees stood over you with trays full of food waiting to sit down, to so thoroughly scrape and then neatly stack dishes according to type and size? And worse still, why did I even bother, since said dishes were headed for the kitchen to be washed anyway? Margaret, the middle-aged dishwasher operator who'd been on the job for more than twenty years and had seen everything, was nonplussed. She'd laugh at me and say that she could always tell when the wheeled-in bus truck to be unloaded was mine. But then I suppose that that was partially my point, my motivation.

I'd like to believe that I, as well as my brother and sister, rightly inherited much of my meticulous nature from my parents, who were always deliberate and orderly, despite the mounting disorder of decades of accumulated things that filled every nook and cranny of our house as well as a metal backyard shed, and a storage locker down the road. Ever meticulous and orderly in the face of all that. Dad in the way he could simultaneously cook elaborate gourmet meals and desserts while keeping the kitchen spanking clean, in the way he mowed and manicured his lawn and crafted his tools, in the way he tended his large vegetable garden. Mom with her penchant for disinfecting surfaces to keep every germ at bay, her taking detailed notes about every aspect of her life and that of significant others even as she was living and observing, her need to save nearly everything that she bought, produced, or simply touched and could claim, just in case.

It pays, of course, to be meticulous when one irons. But I wish I could more completely disavow any connection with some of the metaphoric uses my parents put to the process of ironing. Notably their fondness for the problem-solving and interpersonal expressions: "let's try to iron things out" and "let's just get this ironed out." Those utterances were enough at times to crimp even the most reluctant of rebellious teenager's style. Hearing them, having to soak up their euphemistic-sounding tone, sometimes made me want to escape into another room and scream my head off. I wanted *more* confrontation, dammit, not less, more rough edges, more craziness— even as a part of me sensed how much I feared all that.

Well, not "dammit," exactly, for helping to bolster those well-worn metaphors was the fact that my nonsmoking, essentially teetotaler parents also never cursed, as far as I ever heard—except my mom, famously one time while driving me and my sister to school, exasperated with my sister for some reason, blurting out "you make me so *damn* mad sometimes," shocking the two of us into stunned silence for the remainder of the trip across town.

Cursing simply isn't the morally right, most productive way to express oneself. That's how they might have put it if they'd been so moved to have to explain what they'd consider to be obvious. And since we kids never cursed—well, into our teens maybe, "out in the world," but never in front of them—they were never so moved. And besides, before the thought of any curse, much less its possible utterance, time and place must be given to deep breaths and reason and ways to "iron things out." Which meant that as I was stumbling through early childhood and adolescence, my experience of family fights was less kicking and screaming and more "constructive dialogue," preceded at times by slow burns or stares across rooms or slight but quite definitive turns of the head accompanied by clicks of the tongue, a kind of retort I swear my dad inherited from his mother.

To be sure, there was some passive aggressiveness in some of this, especially on my father's part. But one could also call it civility and respect. And by that I don't mean the gentile or waspish kind. My family wasn't stiff or unduly watchful; neither was my extended family, for the most part. And in that sense, we reflected the larger Black community in which we lived in Anacostia, with its overall sense of connectedness and responsibility. People, of course, acted badly: they fought and there was some crime. But my world was principally, fortunately, not about that.

Once I got to college, though, I began to curse much more freely and even smash a few things more deliberately, although still not in my parents' presence, even though I truly wanted to from time to time. And it felt good, freeing, more improvisational and dangerous, all the cursing and smashing. Felt more me, less them.

Nevertheless...

Geometry

When I was young, I'd sometimes circle my family. In my mind, that is. Or my dreams. Round and round and round I'd go, and where I'd stop... Later, after *Sputnik* and the start of the space race, I'd pretend that I was some satellite, aloft, aloof, both silent and supercharged, a moving marvel in the soaring sky. Everyone looking up in awe at me as I seemed to wander endlessly... Where's he going? they'd cry. And why?

Other times, though, I'd be this point, a kind of pointless point, a dot, a stuck speck in the middle, nearly invisible, forgotten, ever unknowable to them, to everyone, even to me.

Shape-shifting geometry.

Gee, I'm a tree.

Or anything nonhuman, unhuman. Wanting to disappear, to be someplace else, any place else. Or dreaming I had the whole house to myself. Lived alone. Free to do ... who knows what. A loner. A loser. A loose end. With the world all angles and shapes, points and circles, corners and edges around which to peek or hide. Rooms and caverns to enter somewhat fidgety with fear—or, given my ongoing reticence, just never go near.

My own space race.

II

I remember how ecstatic I was when my cousin Gerald helped me and my brother build a two-room hut in our backyard out of found and collected wood and corrugated cardboard, much of it cast off from the famed Curtis Brothers furniture store just two blocks away. All that earnest measuring and shaping, hammering and sawing. Clamps and nails, screws and duct tape. A bit half-cocked in places but quite sturdy, nonetheless.

It wasn't big enough to stand up in, but it was big enough for us to squeeze into, sort of hang out in. Also to defend as some grand fortress when we played knights and warriors up and down and all around the backyards and alleyways with neighborhood boys, swords fashioned out of whatever sticks we could find, rules about mortal wounds or massive defeats as fulsome and fluid as our shouts and cries. We even built a secret space into its floor, sort of underground, where we stored a box of treasures, "secret" valuable things. A treasure chest.

Plus it was a refuge to me during quieter times, a kind of place away without having to go too far away. I even fantasized about living there alone. My space, my place. With my own secret treasures, inside and out. Bravely boxed in and squirreled away... Squared away.

III

"Squared away."

One of my Dad's favorite expressions.

As in: "Let's just get things squared away." As in put in order, arranged in some suitable, proper fashion. Suitable and fine, although the word "fine," if one added a "con," could morph into "confine" in my mind's eye, which could suggest, depending on one's accent and part of speech, either a boundary or an enclosure. Neat and clean and proper. Boxed in, boxed up, suitable for shipping.

And then round and round and round I'd go, circling that expression, searching for an opening, some fatal flaw, some wizardly way to magically "unsquare" it, give it some "untoward" shape, like a half-cocked trapezoid or a rickety ring, with angles and curves, ins and outs.

The geometry of both my sight and my vision.

Besides, "squared away" also projected to me this image of "being a square." As in straitlaced and proper, or just flat-out dull. With a part of me sensing that I already was. All rounded and smooth. No flare-ups, no angles. And then in my head the scenario would be...

My goodness, no angles? Then what are you hiding?

Why, nothing, please, nothing. No thing that I know of. Just boxed in and watched over. Boxed in but not closed.

Okay, fine, then please tell us, what is your bent?

No bent, please, no bent. I'm not bent at all. Just boxed in and squared. Boxed in but not closed.

So then how is one able to access you there?

Why through the door, please, the door. There *is* a door, I swear. With no lock and no key. Just me, only me.

A point turned toothpick, if one shifted POV.
Backed up in a corner,
Hiding in plain sight.
Hence, prone to disappearing
in certain perceived harsh light.
Eyes searching, mind churning,
wondering what shape to others I made,
what private parts poked out,
what creepy contours displayed.

Geometry.
Gee, I'm a...

IV

Plane:

- A flat, two-dimensional surface that extends infinitely.
- The two-dimensional analogue of a point (zero dimensions), a line (one dimension), and three-dimensional space.
- A subspace of some higher-dimensional space, as with a room's wall, infinitely extended.
- A vehicle for a solo flight to ... wherever.

Plane geometry:

- The mathematical study of geometric figures whose parts lie in the same plane, such as polygons, circles, and lines.
- A branch of elementary geometry that deals with plane figures.
- The geometry of figures whose parts all lie in one plane.

I hated plane geometry. Partly because the teacher was old, slow, and boring, but also because I was glumly wrestling with my first year of high school, forever fantasizing about how to both break out and stay within without ... imploding. Besides, after breezing through seventh and eighth grade math all in *one* honor's track seventh-grade year and soaring through the wonderful intricacies of algebra I and II in eighth and ninth grades, plane geometry simply lived up to its, well, homophone. Nevertheless, math—overall my best subject growing up—did pick up for me again throughout the rest of high school with trigonometry, advanced algebra, analytic geometry, and pre-calculus. It was sort of like seventh heaven!

All those precise calculations and acute angles and eureka moments. But then it died for me once and for all when I hit advanced calculus and beyond in college—sent me straight to D-grade hell. The ephemeral numbers, complex theories, cryptic calculations suddenly soaring out or over my head. Not the shapes, though. Never the shapes. The objects on paper or in space. The complex geometry of life now largely away from my parents... Huh.

Geometry.

Gee, I'm...

not a mathematician.

V

Mom was a circle. Dad was a square.
Dad was a drumbeat. Mom was a flare.

Hence, just as I sometimes felt boxed in by Dad,
so did I sometimes feel circled by Mom.
Fearful she'd press me to try something new,
or express what I thought, or *intimately* knew.
Spying round and round
the circumference of her care.

Hence, sometimes I felt challenged
by a double beware.
Encompassed, embraced
by both circle and square.
Driven by drumbeat,
spurred on by flare.
Open up, open up.
Keep in, keep in.
Which way should I go,
which way must I bend?

A bold boxy circle?
A heart-throbbing square?

A black ball in a cube
with little space to spare?

Well, however configured,
I was ever aware,
in unique, discrete
specific sorts of ways,
of the apparent geometry
of my growing-up days.

And so what then,
oh, what would I turn out to be?
What would be the course
of *my* geometry?

Well, this bent, this bend
toward the careening chameleon.
Ever trying and discarding,
fully focused then distracted.
Then baffled, then wanting,
then failing, then running,
then seeking and seeking
again and again.
From engineering to math
to English to acting.
From questioning to straight
to bisexual to gay.
My essence, my pulse,
my being, my way.
Like some wanton shape-shifter,
some self-regarding sphinx.
In ever-pounding search of
some ... evanescent missing link?

VI

It was a trip out of DC and far north along some winding roads
to a town in Maryland almost to the Pennsylvania border. I don't

Author with his father and mother.

remember which one. Perhaps Hagerstown. But then it was my Dad who was driving, and he always seemed to know the way. Just me and my Dad. A late-afternoon trip to attend a program of a Black American Legionnaire organization—a ceremony reserved almost exclusively for me, I think. And my Dad, too, really.

Zooming along in the late afternoon, as I recalled a trip with him months earlier traveling northeast in Maryland rather than west. It was to Morgan State University in Baltimore—a university at which, ironically, I was to be an associate professor of English for just three years, decades later. Arriving there to take some standardized test while Dad would dutifully sit in his car for the time it would take me to take it. My sitting up high and toward the rear of a huge auditorium, my usual choice, for it was there that I could look down and out without risking looking down and out to almost anyone else, all those other seemingly much hipper and cooler Black high school seniors.

And I remember opening the exam packet and zipping, breezing through all the readings and questions and multiple choice answers in English and math, social studies and science. Wondering on occasion what in the world I was missing. Why was I plowing straight through without halting or guessing, looking around once or twice to see if others, too, were breezing. But then no, no, keep your eyes straight ahead. Just keep on keeping on, is what I firmly said. And when I finally emerged and Dad asked me how I did, I said fine, I did okay. Easier than those SATs, I added, as we drove off straight away.

But then later, well, later, it was much more than okay, for I'd gotten the top score on the exam that day and was thus declared the winner of the Legionnaire's scholarship prize. One more scholarship to add to all the others I had won. And hence were we traveling straight toward the setting sun. Straight ahead with such confidence. Just me and my Dad. My faithful, focused, straight-arrow of a dad.

The ceremony itself, though, in some decorated hall—with dinner and speeches and Black folks dressed to the nines, all the glad-handing and

Author with his father.

praise that sometimes boggled my mind, made me want to turn away or half close myself in, except for the veneer of my "shit-eating grin"—well, all that's a blurred moment in my memory, as though some fussy past point I can only squint to see. For that which is most visceral about that long, long day is our heading back home along that two-lane highway, only the headlights of other cars occasionally piercing the late night, and feeling mounting anxiety as Dad began weaving left and right, crossing the center line on the left and toward the guard rails on the right. For he was so tired, so worn out, by work and the stress of straight ahead, which made me wish that *I* was driving us. But what I did instead was to gently touch him and speak out loud to try keeping him awake. And that meant braving some semblance of authority over him for both of our sakes.

Look out, Dad, please be careful.
I'm okay, son, I'm all right.
No, you're not, Dad, you're so tired,
I'd only thought but never said,
as I touched his leg, his knee, his thigh
to keep him moving straight ahead.
Hence, an awkward task did I perform
while striving to suppress my fear.
At odds with how we'd typically connected
through most of my growing up years.
But since we were even closer now
to moving farther apart,
I was glad to be so close to him *then*
that I could feel his drumbeat in my heart.

Straight ahead, son, straight ahead. Then square that corner and straight some more. Directions nearly never shouted—simply whispered from his core. Always working, always doing, shaping a world where we could grow, and then to whatever we said we needed almost never saying, "no." Helping us handle all the twists and turns wherever we or they should go; helping us try squaring all those corners, making everything "just so."

Dad's drumbeat and his square:
pulsing geometry everywhere.
Geometry.
Gee, I'm a...

VII

Well, perhaps one reason for all those years of Mom's "nudging" me with her flare was that she sensed some curbed, inchoate part of *her* lying dormant in *me* somewhere. And thus did she seem to twist and shout when I "burst upon the stage," magically coming onto voice and body, exposing feelings, thoughts, even rage. For after slogging toward some PhD yet forever feeling half empty, I dove headfirst into acting training at the tail end of my twenties.

And with that momentous leap—fueled

Author with his mother.

by a kind of desperate dare—did a follow spot begin to morph out of my mother's pesky flare. A spot at times turned spotlight, continually searching after me, as I grew into this actor whom she wished for all to see. Determined to keep me in the light, that follow spot she kept on, charting my twists and turns, my highs and lows through NYU and beyond. Round and round she'd circle, alerting family and friends, then making flyers, charting buses, handling reservations, payments, loose ends. And with every trip to see me, it was clear that Mom was glad to be firmly in the driver's seat, just as driven as my Dad.

In fact, there was one particular time when she was even *more* driven than he. For it was a time when she took up the *actual* driving, since Dad unfortunately wasn't free. Taking her turn driving one of three cars in a caravan of relatives and friends, on an 800-mile round-trip north—Williamstown, Massachusetts, being the end. It was to see me perform five plays in rep at the theater festival there. And she made the damn best of it for everyone with her usual fun and flair.

And when I turned to *writing* for the stage as well as for TV, she simply supercharged her spot, and continued following me... Pittsburgh, Philadelphia, Baltimore, Seattle, too. One time even a film set at Universal. She seemed to stick to me like glue. Forever urging me—indeed, all us kids—to open wider, explore much more. That was the love light so lodged within her, so fundamental to *her* core.

Mom's circle and her flare:
glistening geometry everywhere.
Geometry.
Gee, I'm a...

VIII

"Every man is an architect of his own future."
Thus reads the quotation that accompanies my smiling photo-

graph in the 1964 Ballou High School yearbook. But I'm not sure why. That is, *I* never said that. In fact, I don't know *who* did. And I don't remember coming across it somewhere and saying, yeah, yeah, that's me, that's me! ... But *someone* had to have chosen it: it didn't just appear. It was *somebody's* attempt to "capture" or "encapsulate" me, class valedictorian, placing those words there as though placing me in some precept, for time immemorial.

Architect...?

IX

When I was in my mid-teens, I found myself obsessing over the "House Plan of the Week," a feature in the Saturday real estate section of *The Washington Post*. Peering at and reading about that chosen house design, and then putting together fifty cents and sending away for my very own copy. And I could hardly wait until they arrived, the odd adrenaline pounding in me as I practically lived by the mailbox, and then when the fat envelope appeared I'd sneak it up to my and my brother's room and, making sure I was alone behind closed doors, carefully open the envelope and unfold the special plans as though they were salacious dirty pictures. But of course, they weren't: they were simply magical blueprints of what seemed to be exotic modern homes. Printed on rather thick paper, as though meant to be cherished and preserved, although I have none of them now. And I'd imagine those designs as my own. Even though I didn't really have any desire to be an architect, per se. For it wasn't about being some master designer, builder: it was about the design itself. The nature of it, the shapes and lines, the angles and measurements, and the way I could *see* the rooms, the structures, all the levels and connections, *imagine* them in three-dimensional space. *That* sort of sensibility. Which was akin to my love of diagramming sentences in grade school—a visual technique for understanding the relationships between parts of speech, long since abandoned in most school curricula. Also, to my acquiring quickly the ability to tie complex knots with lightning speed in the Boy Scouts. Or to my conceiving science fair projects that centered around objects, not chemicals; radio parts or rocket components, not bubbling volcanoes or liquids in test tubes. Or to my love of geography and maps, where I could visually place the places of the world, better keep them in my consciousness, even excelling on the championship Junior ROTC map reading team in high school. Accurately charting things, calculating their relationships, and then seeing them in three-dimensional space.

Dimensions ... shapes ... space...

Geometry.

Gee, I'm a...

X

ARCHITECT:

from Greek: *archi* + *tektōn*

chief artificer

master builder

My father was a master builder, a craftsman. A lifelong machinist by profession and trade, he could create, design, make almost anything it seemed to me. Think it, see it, make it. Cabinets, benches, shelves. Fishing poles, ladles, footrests. Much of such vision and skill learned from observing his own father in his basement, which Dad duplicated in a more formal way when he and Mom finally bought a house of their own and added an addition on the back that had a workshop under the new family room. A shop filled with tools of the craftsman's trade, where he famously designed and constructed a huge, life-size wedding arch out of wood, expertly curved and carved and with its own wood base, for part of the glorious celebration of my sister's wedding. And he made an intricately conceived wooden rocking cradle for his third grandchild that was sturdy enough to work its wondrous way from grandchild to grandchild to even great-grandchild over years. He built a changing table I used for my daughters when they were babies that fit over a waist-high chest of drawers, which he

Author with his father.

also built, and then a few years later when the girls were older he fashioned side by side work desks that stretched over and could fold down beside that chest of drawers to free up space when not in use. He crafted and made and crafted and made as though his mind and his hands were one propulsive, obsessed, creative entity, his plans at times sketched out on pieces of paper, lines and angles sharply drawn, the press of his tools, the screech of his drills and saws, the rush of sandpaper on wood often ringing in my ears as he bent that wood and metal, even plastic at times, to his creative, imaginative, finely focused will.

My mother, in turn, was a chief artificer. In effect, a writer. In fact, one of the most prolific unpublished writers I have ever known. Writing as breathing, with a life of its own. Writing about anything and everything, writing all the time, quietly, unobtrusively but nonetheless compulsively, not only in daily and monthly planners and subject notebooks but also in incredibly detailed travel journals for nearly every one of the dozens of trips, cruises, adventures she went on with family and friends, or the many times she visited children and grandchildren, indelibly noting, marking their every gesture, stride, accomplishment, even after the fact, yet seemingly verbatim at times, as though her mind had some built-in cassette tape forever on record. Bound or spiral or loose-leaf were the accumulating collection of journals, small or large or in between, scattered all over the house, it seemed—perhaps for tacit "safekeeping" or some serendipitous read. Also writing—or actually printing—*everywhere* on practically *anything*. Any random piece of paper that wasn't tied down: the backs of old envelopes, a plethora of post-its, the odd brown paper bag, unused napkins in restaurants. Thank-you notes or praise songs or loving lines to family and friends. Sometimes even set aside unsent, for it was the recorded exhale of expression that seemed to matter most to her. First, second, and third drafts at times, obsessed with being clear, with having just the right words, her eyes and ears ever poised and alert like some reporter suing for some surprising new action, some untold story. Much of her work elegant with image and insight, dazzling and gleaming, although at times a bit innocent, naïve. Letters to the editor, inquiries about offers, notes on appointments or people she'd met, transcriptions of telephone, casual, even overheard conversations. Thoughts and prayers, challenges and achievements. Fond wishes, new discoveries, old finds. All chronicled, preserved, as though she were boxing with Time.

My craftsman Dad, my writer Mom.
Two natural born "architektōns."

Shaping, recording the world
as they saw it.
Reproducing, reimaging the world
as they lived it.
My square of a Dad,
My circle of a Mom.

And so what then, oh what
about little ole me,
my parents' very first progeny?
Some chip off the old block?
Some curve *of* the old ball?
Anything fixed or integrated at all?

Geometry.

Gee, I'm a...
... lover
of language,
of movement,
of story and space,
reaching, stretching
all over the place.
I grow, I shrink,
I slip, I slide,
ever thinking, feeling
how best to open wide.
I forge characters from memory
or sparked by a glance,
some sudden gesture,
some meeting by chance.
I craft tales out of whole cloth
or fragments of speech,
days in the hills,
on the road, even lying
on the beach.
I'm a seeker, a beseecher
of some quiet repute.
I'm a drum, a bass,

a violin, a lute.
I'm the geographer,
choreographer
of my recollected past
and my ongoing living
as I constantly cast
farther and farther
both day and night,
ever playing, shaping,
trying to get things "just right"
for my theater in the round,
my theater in the square,
my theater in my head
virtually everywhere.

I'm...
a rhombus,
a box,
a cube,
a dome.
I'm...
a straight line,
a plane,
a sphere,
a polyhedron.
I'm...
whatever
suggests,
or defines,
my creative home.

Geometry.

Gee, I'm...
more and more
... me.

Flux: An Afterword

I

One of the first things I look out for whenever I drive across the Anacostia River via the 11th Street Bridge and head up Martin Luther King, Jr. Avenue into my old neighborhood is "The World's Largest Chair." It's still there. Right at V Street. Nineteen and a half feet tall, 4,600 pounds when it was made of solid mahogany, it was built in 1959 in honor of the thriving Curtis Brothers Furniture Store in front of which it so boldly stood. Stood, because although the chair is still there—rebuilt to the same height but this time out of 2,500 pounds of aluminum after the weather-damaged original chair was removed—the Curtis Brothers store is long gone.

Other things in the neighborhood are also long gone, of course.

Kresge's, just up Good Hope Road, was a five and ten cent store (which eventually morphed into Kmart). My brother, sister, and I would joyously and urgently race up and down its aisles a couple of days before Christmas, clutching the money we'd saved and/or been given by our parents to buy presents for them and each other. We would stealthily check out what we could afford and pay for it without letting anyone but the cashier see, which was no small feat in a medium-sized store.

The Anacostia movie theater, farther up Good Hope, built in

1947, closed and demolished in 1967, was off-limits to us until the mid–1950s, before which we were restricted to the local theater for colored people, the George Washington Carver. Or else we had to travel elsewhere, notably uptown to the Lincoln, Republic, or Booker T. on the bustling "Black" U Street.

The Little Tavern, with its Tudor cottage style resembling a quaint little take-out place in an urban fairytale, used to sit right near the bridge. At the Little Tavern we could not only buy great-tasting regular hamburgers but also "buy them by the bag"—six cute, silver-dollar-sized ones.

The Miles Long Sandwich Shop, at Pleasant and Maple View, was the place where on special occasions we'd order take-out food of delicious half and whole submarine sandwiches, and even get the more expensive steak with cheese and fried onions if we, or Mom and Dad, had "extra" money.

Long gone.

But the giant chair remains as an enduring local landmark.

I could never just casually pass by it when I was a kid—that chair—even if I was in a hurry to be somewhere. It was too outsized to be ignored. I was *compelled* to look again for the millionth time, in some ways as though it were the first. I often wondered what it would be like to "sit" in it. To be able to look down on the neighborhood from that vantage point, as though the chair were by rights all mine and I was big enough to get in it without assistance. Me as the Friendly Black Giant of Anacostia!

Anacostia… Anacostia transforming, changing, promise ever in the air. Visions of a sparkling new waterfront and trendy shops, office buildings and more goods and services, new housing of all sorts for all kinds of folks, all dancing in the heads of elected officials, savvy business people, focused community activists. From Busboys and Poets to MahoganyBooks to the Anacostia Arts Center to Martha's

Table, the neighborhood continues to evolve. Why there's even a Starbucks just up and across from Big Chair.

For after all, everyone wants proper attention to be paid, especially if neglect has been heretofore rampant. Everyone is in favor of needed improvements—solid job opportunities, sounder schools, safer streets. But "improvements" at what price for those still rooted in the community? Especially those with deep roots, however planted and shaped over the years? Anacostia: the once Native American trading center; the once planned white suburb of old Washington City; the once promised land for post–Civil War free Blacks aching for release from their miserable central-city alley dwellings; the once home-ownership capital of the nation's capital; the once ... the now...

II

When I don't drive—that is, when I walk—or more precisely when I *walk out* onto Howard Road, having gotten off the DC metro at the Anacostia station, what I immediately glimpse is the majestic Thurgood Marshall Academy, set back from the street by a verdant lawn. Its formal address is on the northern stretch of the long Martin Luther King, Jr. Avenue, by which I mean Nichols Avenue, by which I mean Monroe Street, by which I mean Asylum Road, by which I mean Bladensburg-Piscataway Road, by which I mean perhaps some trail through the land of the Nacotchtank or Nacostine Native Americans. Their land, that is, before white folks landed, explored, cajoled, seized, and employed many of their "re's" (repurpose, remove, re-assess, repackage) in whatever order has suited them from the early 1600s on. They claimed more and more land because they could smell it, see it, stand on it, with a cocky bully's "it ain't yours just 'cause you're here" attitude and with the aid of two other powerful weapons: guns and disease. That stellar high school academy, of course, is essentially housed, anchored, rooted in the refurbished old Birney School, built more than a century ago for Black kids in this community formerly known as Hillsdale. The neighborhood was initially set apart, tacitly walled off, from Uniontown to the slight northeast, which was planned out and built for working class white folks in the 1850s and officially named Anacostia in 1886, partially because, well, there were so many post–Civil War Union Towns all around the nation. Hillsdale was later set apart from Barry Farms to the slight southwest, which was a community for working class *Black* folks developed beginning in the late 1860s on land purchased by the Freedmen's Bureau from the Barry family. The Barrys had purchased a part of the Saint Elizabeths land tract, initially for speculation and profit and then for "farming." Hillsdale was briefly called Potomac City, though others wanted to name it Hillsboro, a name Frederick Douglass supposedly objected to because it reminded him of the area on Maryland's eastern shore from which he'd escaped as a slave. Hillsdale/Barry Farms remained a segregated community of striving Black folks along the Anacostia River until the capital city government decided in the 1940s to build the Suitland Parkway, mostly to connect disparate military bases and federal office buildings, eschewing any concern for the interests of the Black community that parkway would cut right through and disrupt. This meant that middle-class Black homeowners were now physically separated from Black folks in the largely public-housing-occupied Barry Farm Dwellings, erected after some of the single-family homes Black folks worked so hard to build by themselves after the Civil War had been torn down via eminent domain to make way for real estate speculators to pop in and build cheap public housing backed by 90 percent loan guarantees from the newly formed National Housing Authority. You see, post–Depression folks were desperate for housing and the whole of Anacostia's slightly rolling hills were more "conducive" to such public housing/apartment zoning and building than

DC "proper"—the same "proper" DC which didn't initially plan for the new Metro system built in the 1980s to even *stop* in then "public housing-riddled" Ward Eight, but to go straight from the pristine National Mall to the Maryland suburbs. That would have meant that I *wouldn't* have been able to get off at an Anacostia Metro Station and step out to view that wonderfully restored-looking old Birney School building, where my Dad went to school through the eighth grade before heading out to Armstrong High School across the Anacostia River since the neighborhood Anacostia High School, opened in 1935 and an easy walk for him, was closed to colored kids. I went to old Birney, too, for kindergarten, until the new Birney opened in 1950 across Suitland Parkway and smack dab at the virtual entrance to Barry Farm Dwellings at Sumner Road and Nichols Avenue, although those dwellings, too, have been dismantled, raised, torn down in preparation for some sort of "a mixed-use, mixed income community." And *that* Birney Elementary School has recently been refurbished and now shines brightly as Excel Academy: Washington's first Public School for Girls...

I am walking along Shannon Place now, past the rear of old, old Birney School / new Marshall Academy to my right, past the Revival Temple Church, in a space where formerly lay Saint Phillip's Episcopal Chapel, to my left, past the "low-slung" modern Savoy Elementary School to my right, and up to that second home Grandpa Frazier had built in 1936 to my left. All the while I'm eyeing, in the next block farther down on my right, the first home Grandpa Frazier had built in 1916, which is where I grew up in the 1950s and 60s. But then I suddenly stop, swivel around, and peer back down Shannon Place toward the Metro Station and observe what I'd previously only cursorily noted: that the street's former exit onto Howard Road is now permanently blocked, sealed off, creating a kind of cul-de-sac. What brings that fact pointedly home to me is a "NO OUTLET" traffic sign at the corner of Shannon Place and Talbert Street, separating the stretch of Shannon Place on which my family lived into two blocks. No outlet, that is, for cars. That warning sign certainly doesn't prevent me from *walking* back to the Anacostia Metro stop, ending my attempt to somehow walk back in *time*, back to a time when the street was essentially all Black, before the most recent "encroachment." The new Metro stop at now cul-del-sacked Shannon Place and Howard Road means that folks can be relatively close to white collar work in the City proper across the river. So then why not buy some Victorian-era house on Shannon Place to spruce up or renovate, peacefully live in, while perhaps lobbying the powers that be to keep the new neighborhood "just so"? In any event, papers have now been officially filed to expand the Anacostia Historic District to include Shannon Place in order that new folks buying up and moving in can't just willy-nilly tear down hundred-year-old homes to build sleek, modern condos. Rather, they must creatively modernize within without "defacing" the exterior character of the existing Washington Row–style row houses and Colonial Revival–style single family dwellings that make the new Anacostia worth living in in the first place. Or second, or third ... as the "re's" just keep on rolling...

Nonetheless, I walk on, my three-quarters-of-a-century self picturing my tenth-of-a-century self running up and down the streets and alleys, or speeding along on my first two-wheeled bicycle, which I spruced up with sleek silvery paint to make it seem like some sort of super speed bike, clipping a plastic playing card with a clothespin onto the back wheel's spokes to make a sharp clacking sound as I rode up and down and all around, announcing to everybody that they should just get out of the way 'cause Kermit's here!

Back then anyway. For how *now* am I here? And what now *is* this here? ...

As I walk, curious, the street feels abandoned by kids, by families. Or perhaps it's just in my head, in my sense of things in the mid-morning hour. A neighborhood seemingly bereft of the kind of kid-filled families I grew up with. Some slight, inchoate whiff of "gentle" gentrification hanging in the air perhaps. I don't know. What I *do* know is that I'm rightly more stranger than neighbor now, more alien than native, more "used to be" than "is." And least here ... now. A divorced gay Black man with a thriving family and a rich, enduring heritage of his own... A writer—among other disparate things— walking, remembering, seeing anew.

July 2021